6/04

# GROWING
## YOUR COMPANY'S
# LEADERS

# GROWING
## YOUR COMPANY'S
# LEADERS

How Great Organizations Use
Succession Management to
Sustain Competitive Advantage

## ROBERT M. FULMER
### AND JAY A. CONGER

**AMACOM**

American Management Association

New York • Atlanta • Brussels • Chicago • Mexico City • San Francisco
Shanghai • Tokyo • Toronto • Washington, D.C.

This publication is designed to provide accurate and authoritative information in regard to the subject matter covered. It is sold with the understanding that the publisher is not engaged in rendering legal, accounting, or other professional service. If legal advice or other expert assistance is required, the services of a competent professional person should be sought.

Various names used by companies to distinguish their software and other products can be claimed as trademarks. AMACOM uses such names throughout this book for editorial purposes only, with no intention of trademark violation. All such software or product names are in initial capital letters or ALL CAPITAL letters. Individual companies should be contacted for complete information regarding trademarks and registration.

Library of Congress Cataloging-in-Publication Data

Fulmer, Robert M.
    Growing your company's leaders : how great organizations use succession management to sustain competitive advantage / Robert M. Fulmer, Jay A. Conger.
        p.   cm.
    Includes index.
    ISBN 0-8144-0767-6
    1. Executives.   2. Leadership.   3. Executive succession.   4. Executive succession—Case studies.   I. Conger, Jay Alden.   II. Title.

HD38.2.F85   2004
658.4'07128—dc22

                                                                2003015834

Printing number

10   9   8   7   6   5   4   3   2   1

# CONTENTS

# PREFACE AND ACKNOWLEDGMENTS

For decades, succession management has been considered one human resources system that every company needed. Its primary purpose was to identify replacements for senior executives who would eventually depart the organization through death or retirement. In many companies, it ended up a largely mechanical process. It was one of several "annual events"—"time to fill out those succession planning forms." The possibility that it might be deployed for genuine development or for retention of talented individuals was to a large extent untapped. Instead, it was treated more like a life insurance policy—we all know we need it, but we would rather not talk about the events that are likely to make it necessary. The assumption was that top managers were in place for the duration until some accident or health problem might remove them. It was rare to think about the top person being lured away by another company.

This book explores how the competition for talent is changing and reports on what some leading firms have done to use succession management as a source of strategic advantage.

## The Study Sources

The information and recommendations in this book are based on the work of the authors in a landmark study for the American

Productivity and Quality Center (APQC) conducted in 2001, with updated information for this book researched and added by the authors. To discover what leading practitioners of this complex art had learned, sixteen sponsors embarked on a journey to learn from such best practice organizations as Dell Computer, Dow Chemical Company, Eli Lilly and Company, PanCanadian Petroleum, and Sonoco Products Company. Since the study, we have added Bank of America, given its strong reputation in the field of succession management. The authors of this book participated as subject matter experts in a study of succession management systems conducted by the American Productivity & Quality Center. APQC is a consortium focused on identifying business best practices and innovative methods of transferring those practices.

A group of other leading organizations served as *sponsors*, providing support and data and receiving early access to the valuable findings of the study. These included AARP, Amgen, Celanese Chemical, City Public Service of San Antonio, Compaq Computer Corporation, Deere & Company, Discover Financial Services, Department of Veterans Affairs–VBA, Department of Veterans Affairs–VHA, Intel, Internal Revenue Service, Lutheran Brotherhood, Mattel, Occidental Petroleum Corporation, Office of the U.S. Comptroller of the Currency, and the Panama Canal Authority.

Several organizations that were believed to have achieved a high degree of success in succession management were identified by the research team and invited to participate in the study. Based on the results of screening interviews and company willingness to participate, a final list of five *partners* was selected by the sponsors. These "best practice partners" were Dell Computer, Dow Chemical Company, Eli Lilly and Company, PanCanadian Petroleum, and Sonoco Products Company.

Because Bank of America succession management had been

benchmarked by the original APQC panel, the authors collected information from them as part of the follow-up research.

Through a detailed set of questions and site visits, the APQC study team sought to determine how best practice organizations were managing to tie succession activities to their organizational culture and challenges. The study team also explored links between succession management and company leadership development processes. More about this methodology is contained in Appendix B of this book.

The origins and evolution of succession management were major foci of the APQC investigation. The participating best practice organizations openly described their methods of developing top management support and overcoming the ever present time constraints that consistently war against the successful identification, tracking, and development of future leaders.

The study personnel were Lou Cataline, APQC, project lead; Alice Haytmanek, APQC, team member; Darcy Lemons, APQC, team member; Robert M. Fulmer, Ph.D., subject matter expert; Jay A. Conger, DBA, study adviser; and Dr. James M. Kouzes, study adviser. Our appreciation is expressed to the APQC team and to APQC president, Carla O'Dell, for her leadership in the development of a unique approach to best practice research and for allowing us to share this research with a wider audience. We also appreciate the insights and patience of Adrienne Hickey, our editor at AMACOM, as well as the editorial assistance of Dale Berryhill and Charlie Walton.

The focus of the study was to draw on input from the subject matter expert team and secondary research literature. The APQC study team identified four scope areas for research. These areas guided the design of the data collection instruments and were critical in guiding the progress of the study. The scope areas were similar to the chapters contained in this manuscript. We have also provided detailed case studies of the benchmark firms (Appendix A). While some of this data is included in the initial sections of the book, we felt that many readers would be interested in getting a complete picture of the individual firms and their approaches to succession management. We are most appreciative to all of the "best practice partners" for allowing us access to work that has taken them years to develop. We would especially like to thank Brian Fishel and Jim Shanley of Bank of America, Belinda Hyde of Dell, Steve Constantin and Frank Morgan of Dow Chemical, Mark Ferrara and Laura Dorsey of Lilly, Belinda Austin of PanCanadian, and Rick Maloney and Allan McLeland at Sonoco. While we have attempted to update the data collected in the original research as we go to press, successful succession management is not a static target. Outstanding practices stay outstanding by continuously being refined and adapted to meet changing circumstances. Consequently, the reader is encouraged to view the account of these "best practices" and case histories as artifacts that may provide reference points to help address some of the challenges they may be experiencing.

# Chapter One

# Succession Management: The New Imperative

Few firms are truly prepared for what has come to be called the "War for Executive Talent." Historically, the population for this stratum of management has grown in concert with overall economic activity (Gross Domestic Product). If economic growth continues at a modest 2 percent for the next decade and a half, this would result in a need for a third more senior leaders than there are today. Yet the supply of the age cohort that has traditionally provided entrée into the executive ranks (35–44 year olds) is actually declining in the United States and will have dropped by 15 percent between 2000 and 2015 because of the difference in the size of the baby boom generation and the much smaller Generation X. With impending retirements for baby boomer executives over the decade, most large companies will have to scramble to meet gaps in senior leadership talent.

Not only will there be a shortfall in the overall size of the executive talent pool, but there will also be important shortages in the types of background experiences required for tomorrow's senior leaders. For example, the global and more dynamic economy of this century will require executive talent with a more complex skill set than ever before. Leaders will need greater technological literacy, a sophisticated understanding of global marketplaces, fluency in multiple cultures, entrepreneurial skills, extensive networks of varied relationships, changing leadership skills, and the ability to lead in increasingly "delayered, disaggregated, and virtual" organizations. Few companies have sufficient, well-honed internal initiatives to develop such capabilities. Instead, executive development is more often a haphazard and opportunistic set of uncoordinated events. The price to be paid for this is a serious shortage of executive leadership talent—shallow bench strength.

One visible symptom of this growing problem is the rise in "outsider" CEO candidates at many Fortune 1000 firms as well as the high failure rates of CEOs in recent years. Unable to groom effective internal candidates, companies are turning to a handful of firms that are more successful at development. In many ways, however, this approach is a short-term fix for deeper, more systemic problems. The high CEO failure rate suggests that developmental experiences at many companies are too narrow or too "fast-tracked," producing executives who do not possess sufficient breadth and strategic grounding to lead their firms in more challenging environments.

Exacerbating this looming talent shortage is the greater mobility that successful managers and executives possess today. Over the last two decades, search firms have risen in size and power as the movers and brokers of talent. The research arms of the leading search firms proactively compile vast directories of management talent and track the latest changes in the organizational charts to see who might be available for opportunities. Each year, they move thousands of managers across companies in every industry. In addition, career opportunities around the world can now be easily identified on company Internet sites. Job posting sites such as Monster.com have enhanced the visibility of opportunities and, in turn, mobility. As a result, many small- and medium-size companies can now target the same kinds of talent—a capability that has been historically reserved for large firms with dedicated recruiting departments. For the younger generations, these somewhat smaller firms can provide greater opportunities for increased responsibility, impact, and wealth—making them as attractive as or more so than Fortune 500 corporations.

Feeding into these facilitators of mobility is a change in attitudes among the younger generations of managers—the product of the destruction of the old "loyalty contract" between companies and their employees so characteristic of the 1950s and 1960s. Having watched their parents being laid off in the late 1980s and 1990s, Generation X members have little sense of corporate loyalty. Their belief is that loyalty is no longer rewarded. Instead, it is assumed that only by moving among different firms can one gain greater rewards and responsibility. In other words, opportunities for upward mobility are seriously hampered by remaining in a single firm over a career. This belief, aided by search firms and the Internet, has accelerated company-hopping. Today, the average executive will have worked in five organizations, and that number may increase to seven by 2010.

In response to the challenges surrounding leadership talent, old management systems are being reinvented. The contemporary concern with both guarding one's talent and developing its capabilities to the fullest has led to the rediscovery and redesign of the old human resources systems. Much more than "de-sexing" the old time "manning charts," the new forms of *succession management* bring a revival of certain old concepts but with critical differences. Before we explain these essential differences, it is helpful to revisit the old systems to understand what they attempted to accomplish. From there, we can trace their evolution to today.

## The Old Ways

As noted in the preface, succession management has traditionally been considered a necessary human resources system for every company. Its primary purpose was to identify replacements for senior executives who would eventually depart the organization. Companies rarely considered the possibility that it might be deployed for genuine development or for retention of talented individuals. The assumption was that top managers were in place for the duration, until some accident or health problem might remove them.

So most companies possessed an essential, but largely unheralded, succession management list. It was the paper version of private, top-level discussions concerning probable successors to the corporate throne. The corporate succession list was to ensure that some thought had been given to identifying an adequate and appropriate pool of replacements. They would be warmed up and ready, should any of the top players leave the playing field.

These older models of succession management had several fundamental shortcomings. For example, their primary focus was not on development but on replacement. They were most often referred to as "candidate slates" or "managing charts." For example, in 1967, the stated purpose of General Electric's Corporate

Executive Manpower Staff list was, "The development and timely availability of thoroughly experienced, competent, and proven general managers for the Company's top positions." In this description, we see the characteristics of the early succession management systems. They were focused only on the very top positions of the company. As a result, the names on the list were chosen at the general manager level. Secondly, they gave top management few options in the search for next generations of leadership. Managers were told, "Here's the list—take your pick—no options for looking beyond the list or asking why these names appear." So succession management in the 1960s basically equated to executive replacement. And, rather than having a *developmental* focus, success was measured by the maintenance of a list of individuals ready to move up the corporate ladder.

These earlier systems were also quite formal. People had to create very detailed and quite rigid replacement lists or *slates*. The process often felt bureaucratic. As a participant, you were moved methodically after a certain number of years from one step to the next step. So, while you might prove to be a fast learner and a high performer, you still had to stay within the lock step of the career path. Ownership was isolated within the senior levels of the operating units or at corporate headquarters. There was complete secrecy in the sense that only the most senior people knew who stood where on the list. Knowledge about when and how career moves would be accomplished was limited to the executive levels of an organization. The notion that succession systems could be beneficial below the executive level was not even considered.

## The Reinvention

Beginning in the late 1980s, many corporations became deeply interested in leadership development. The initial wave of development activities, however, focused primarily on training and education. Managers were sent off to business school programs, or trainers came into companies to teach leadership skills. As the popularity of these programs grew, there was a concern that leadership development had positioned itself around a set of "one-time educational events." Meanwhile, research at the Center for Creative Leadership in Greensboro, North Carolina, demonstrated that jobs and bosses were often the best places to develop leadership talent.[1] Concern therefore grew that educational interventions were insufficient in themselves to support genuine leadership development. Attention turned toward succession planning, with the possibility that such systems could be reinvented as a tool to support development. The hope was that succession systems could be redeployed to move leadership development efforts beyond simply training toward a longer term perspective, where jobs and bosses became the essential ingredients in developing leadership capability.

This reinvention in succession management as a mechanism for identifying and cultivating leadership talent has occurred only in the last several years. Until recently, most companies organized their leadership development and succession management activities into separate silos. As a result, succession management languished in the shadows of leadership development, due, in part, to the limitations identified earlier. A few farsighted firms, however, realized the power and potential of succession planning systems that were well aligned with other aspects of leadership development. In other words, a number of firms began to realize that the two were not separate activities but potentially one and the same.

Today, we are witnessing the impact of this emerging new breed of succession systems. For example, contemporary systems no longer think solely about the *replacement* of talent. They are also focused on *development*. These new systems offer greater potential to leadership developers. They take a more systemic perspective toward the organization's talent and strategy. More and more of the emphasis is on the candidate's potential rather than simply on recent performance. For example, greater attention is now given to how a certain assignment might develop the potential of an individual. Replacement lists are much more fluid and function as talent pools rather than as "slates." Ownership is more widely distributed throughout the firm. The most effective systems are now owned and championed by the senior operating executives of the company, often in concert with the board of directors. At the same time, operating executives and general managers throughout the organization play active ownership roles as well.

At the present, thanks to technology, the normal succession planning system is as simple (and as dynamic) as an Excel spreadsheet. Most systems are highly technologically enabled. The forces that drove the reinvention of succession systems have also produced systems with greater simplicity. In spite of a business model that emphasizes technology, Dell has actually reduced the computerized emphasis of its succession planning process to make it easier for managers in remote locations to participate with ease and efficiency.

And, where the old systems were characterized by complete confidentiality and secrecy, today's systems actually encourage a lot of involvement by individuals who are participants and candidates. Individual candidates may not have access to all the data in their individual records, but they are more involved and receive detailed and candid feedback. In a few companies, there is actual transparency about where a candidate stands in the succession system. In contrast, under the older systems, few participants knew where they actually stood in terms of their potential for career opportunities ahead.

This broadened approach is in part the result of the realization in the 1990s that leadership meant much more than just having a strong CEO or executive team. Companies began to act in accordance with their realization that the development of leadership talent had to be consistent and on-going from the top to the bottom in their organization. The more effective succession systems became the mechanisms for disciplining the organization to search for and prepare leadership talent at every level. Today, forward-looking firms are building their serious efforts at leadership development through their succession management systems.

## Why the Renewed Interest Today?

The forces that have renewed interest in succession systems and have changed them in dramatic ways are trends that have affected business in the new global economy. First, leadership is—and has always been—a relatively scarce commodity within companies. Even after decades of interest in the identification and development of talent, effective leaders are a rare asset. To lose a strong leader is a serious blow to any organization. McKinsey Consulting named the resulting fray the "war for talent,"[2] and despite the economic downturn and severe corporate downsizings of the last few years it is a very real and serious war. Corporations that fail to hold their talented employees when competitors or other opportunities come courting are sure to be the losers.

Second, the leading players in the workforces of corporations today tend to be the *knowledge* workers. Knowledge workers are those who, as Peter Drucker likes to say, carry their expertise "between their ears." What they have to offer is brainpower; and, as Drucker adds, knowledge workers "have two legs"—in other words, they can walk out the door. In the arenas in which competitive advantage is more dependent on specialization and knowledge, talent becomes much more precious but at the same time more mobile.

Third, employee "contracts" centered on performance entered the employment picture in the 1980s and then accelerated in the 1990s. They were in large part the outcome of a hypercompetitive business environment that required outstanding company performance to ensure success. The old "lifetime employment for loyalty" contract was destroyed by the massive layoffs of this era, which undermined the traditional notion that employees could count on lifetime employment as long as they were loyal citizens. In the 1990s, companies like General Electric basically substituted performance contracts for the antiquated assumption that there was any such thing as corporate loyalty. GE's concept was that the top third of employees were performance stars, the middle two-thirds needed work, and the bottom ten percent would eventually be forced out due to poor performance. This attitude, which now pervades many corporations, has totally changed the employment contract and put greater demands on companies to be more transparent about how they define performance. At the same time, many companies now feel that they must proactively provide opportunities that develop their high potentials into high performers.

Given the demise of the loyalty contract, the new employment contract says, in effect that, "If you are a high performer, we will keep giving you great opportunities." In a similar vein, some firms are saying, "We can't guarantee you continued employment, but we will provide developmental experiences that will guarantee your employability." An effective succession management system can allow a company to be more disciplined about identifying great opportunities and identifying employees who deserve and need those great opportunities at given junctures.

The fourth factor driving renewed interest in succession systems is the Internet. This technology has enhanced the mobility of leadership talent. As we noted earlier, new tools like Monster.com have made it easy for talented people to log onto a clearinghouse for talent and find interesting and better job opportunities. The increased ease and speed with which outside opportunities can come calling on a company's prized players have made clear the premium that is placed on talent.

Fifth, executive recruiters and headhunters today possess greater clout and sophistication. No longer is it considered "ungentlemanly" to recruit your competitor's employees. When the outside world came raiding, relentlessly trying to find, contact, and lure knowledge workers, the value on those workers (and keeping them) rose dramatically. The dollar value of knowledge workers created an entire industry devoted to stealing good people away from other companies.

Finally, an additional force that has brought succession management front and center and encouraged its transformation has been nonstop, unpredictable, organizational change. Change has always been the one constant of human endeavor—now it just comes at us twice as fast as it used to. Shifts in the environment cause shifts in critical competences within organizations and leave companies with less and less ability to predict the types of talent they are going to need. As a result, organizations today have to quickly identify growing gaps in talent as well as emerging needs for new types of talent. Well designed succession management systems have the power to provide advance notice of where talent gaps might be looming, what talent needs might be emerging, and even where talent gaps could appear unexpectedly.

As a byproduct of these forces, alert organizations today are deeply concerned about talent retention and development. One of the promises of the new generation of succession systems is their ability to harness talent by programming a continuous stream of challenges and job assignments. A good succession management system can monitor the progress of a specific candidate and, when indicated, propose time in a new role that will keep that candidate challenged and growing. Organizations can now take a more disciplined view of where promising individuals are in their careers. Are they getting sufficient developmental opportunities and the right bosses? What would be the ideal next job assignment? What experiences are needed to round out their skill set and to prepare them for new leadership roles? The reinvented succession management system is one of the corporation's best tools today for talent retention and development.

## The Purpose of Effective Succession Management Systems

The purpose of a highly effective succession management system is two-fold. The first purpose is to serve the needs of the organization by helping to provide a continuous and deep supply of talent. For example, many companies that grew rapidly in the 1990s discovered that they had growing gaps of internal talent. Today, many of the talent gaps are associated with the impending retirement of aging baby boomer executives. In addition, the more proactive firms realize that talent gaps are being continually produced by fundamental shifts in their business environments, which produce demands for new skill sets or capabilities.

In contrast, the more reactive firms have made costly mistakes as they push poorly prepared, underdeveloped managers into new roles. Often, they end up having to hire outsiders for management roles, which solves one problem but may create several others. For example, there are problems caused by the "slow learning ramp time" that these outsiders require. In addition, newcomers may dilute or distort valued corporate culture and traditions.

The ideal succession system helps corporations plan for such emerging needs. The best systems not only fill talent gaps but, as importantly, retain talent. They also powerfully clarify performance standards. An effective system forces the organization to be very clear about what standards and competencies will be used for measuring and rewarding talent. Managers in the succession pool get clear messages about what types of performance are and will be rewarded.

The second aim of an effective succession management system is to serve the employees. Individual high performers will always have external opportunities to go elsewhere. An effective succession management system helps to keep them challenged and motivated to prevent job-hopping to those external opportunities. In addition, many companies have historically suffered from poor utilization of their talent. High performers who are stuck in jobs they perceive as inadequate become prime targets for headhunters. The most effective succession system helps individuals to develop potential by timely moves to opportunities that match their needs and complement their current skill set. The best systems provide a continual stream of challenging opportunities as well as candid and constructive developmental feedback on performance and potential. An effective system can enable highly talented people to move on a faster, or at least, more appropriate, track.

## Characteristics of Best Practice Approaches

In this book, we look at the essential components of an effective succession system. We examine how "succession savvy" corporations have built their systems and how they have maintained high levels of support for them. We also show how their succession systems develop the right types and amounts of leadership talent. As a "preview of coming attractions," we summarize below several of the traits that characterize the approaches of these best practice leaders in succession management:

*First, the most effective systems are simple and easy to use.* All participants—not just those running the systems but candidates as well—have easy access to them. Data is secure but open to those who need it. The winning systems are nonbureaucratic, uncomplicated processes. As an element of that simplicity, there is a unified approach to succession management to ensure consistency and to maintain objectivity of succession management between different business units, organizational levels, and geographic areas.

*Second, the best systems are developmentally oriented rather than simply focused or replacement oriented.* System processes are clearly more concerned with the continuing growth and development of the employee than with an *ultimate* job title. They introduce a discipline into the organization that continually reminds everyone that leadership development and talent retention are critical priorities and every manager's responsibility. The system becomes a proactive vehicle for managers and executives to reflect on the progress of their talent and the opportunities they require for genuine development.

*Third, highly effective systems always actively involve the very top players of the organization.* The CEO and the executive team are committed sponsors and champions—proactively participating in determinations of talent and in "next steps" to ensure the maximum development of their talented employees. Effective succession management is seen as a critical strategic tool by senior executives for attracting and retaining their most talented leaders.

*Fourth, best practice succession systems are effective at spotting gaps in talent and at identifying important "linchpin" positions.* They highlight existing or emerging needs where there are potential shortages of talent within the firm. They focus intensively on linchpin positions—a select set of jobs that are critical to the overall success of the organization. These positions and the individuals who fill them merit and receive regular and intensive attention. The better systems also identify the best jobs for development and whether there are a sufficient number of these or shortages.

*Fifth, succession planning still does the job of monitoring the succession process, enabling the company to make certain that the right people are moving into the right jobs at the right time and that gaps are being spotted early.* The best systems incorporate frequent checkpoints throughout the year. These checkpoints monitor who is where and where the person should be going next. A checkpoint function is built into the system to spot a problem *before* it becomes a problem! Succession management is so important that the best practitioners don't ignore this function for even a quarter.

*Finally, the most successful systems are built around continual reinvention.* One of the clearest insights from our research is that effective succession management is a journey, not a destination. Best practice companies did not succeed in their first efforts at succession management. Similarly, none have rested on their laurels since having their process up and running. They continually refine and adjust their systems as they receive feedback from line executives and participants, monitor developments in technology, and learn from other leading organizations. To avoid the ever-present danger of becoming bureaucratized and mechanical, best practice systems therefore actively incorporate dialogues and debates about talent and about the succession process. There are continuous "conversations" about what is needed for the future of each candidate, about who should be where, and when. There are continuous conversations on the part of the guardians and designers about the planning process and how its utilization can be improved.

# The Key Dimensions of an Effective System

Throughout this book, we consider a set of key dimensions that characterize succession systems that successfully promote leadership development. To establish a map for our journey together, we will introduce these essential dimensions here in brief. These components form an ecosystem—in other words, they reinforce and support each other. A failure to appreciate their interrelationships can lead to a flawed succession system.

## *Corporate Strategy*

At the bedrock of any succession system must be the company's strategy, both its *marketplace* strategy and its *talent* strategy. Succession management occupies a key position as an interface between the human resources function and the strategic direction of an organization. In this role, it is a vital resource in anticipating the future needs of the organization in terms of finding, assessing, developing, and monitoring the human capital required by the

organization's strategy. In designing any effective succession management system, several key questions must therefore be asked.
What are the strategic objectives of the company in terms of marketplaces and geography? What are the implications of that strategy for talent needs and development and for performance
standards? In turn, what will be the talent strategies of the firm—
attraction, retention, and development? And how do we translate
these into our succession systems?

For this "translation" to work, there has to be a close partnership between the senior executive ranks and the human resources
function. They must be partners in understanding what the business strategy is and in preparing company talent to meet the demands of that strategy. Together, they must provide answers to
such critical questions as, "What types of leadership and talent
capabilities will be needed as we enter new markets or geographies
or grow and reinvent our existing businesses? What is the current
state and availability of individuals with these capabilities? What
types of developmental assignments will be needed most in the
future as the firm unfolds its strategy ahead?" While serving as
trusted adviser and confidant of the CEO, the succession management teams must also reflect the concerns and needs of line executives and managers throughout the business units. The latter
may have a greater appreciation for emerging threats and opportunities and their implications for the firm's talent strategy.

## Sponsors and Owners

The sponsors and owners of any succession system are critical to
its usefulness and acceptance. Sponsorship has to be at the very
top, both at the top of the corporation and at the top of functions
and operating units. All the best practice companies we studied

felt fortunate to have the enthusiastic support of top management. But this support was not gratuitous; instead, it was earned
by providing an essential service to the executives. At other best
practice companies, the CEO is the key sponsor for succession
management, and a senior management committee of vice presidents actively stewards the process at the corporate level. Ideally,
the board of directors is also involved. The board itself needs to
be knowledgeable about succession candidates at the executive
level.

The ownership of the system is usually shared among the business heads (along with HR, which traditionally has been the
owner of the processes and tools but today also serves as the system's guardian for the CEO). At the same time, line management
owns the deliverables and is held accountable for the outcomes of
the succession process. HR is held accountable for the system design and its effectiveness as a design and as a process. Periodic
reviews by the senior executives and divisional heads can insure
that the system continues to reflect the needs of the corporation.

## Talent Identification and Talent Pools

The third dimension is the selection or identification of talent.
Succession systems base their assessments directly on performance
results, the individual's potential, and a set of leadership and organizational competencies valued by the organization. In some
cases, there is no universal competency model for the entire organization, but, rather there are several models, which reflect varia-
tions in demands by function and level. That said, best practice
companies tend to use fewer competencies in their models, feeling
that simplicity and focus are stronger advantages than comprehensive efforts. For example, Dow has moved from having differ-

ent competencies for each global business to a common set of
seven used throughout the corporation. Ideally, these models also
contain "derailing attributes" that provide a set of red flags to
participants or reminders of the types of behaviors to avoid. In
addition to competencies, there are tiered assessments of the
readiness of an individual to be moved into the next position.
These are staggered by "readiness today," "readiness in the near
future," and "readiness a year or two down the road." For the
very top positions, there are position-specific determinations for
individual participants, but for the levels below, there are talent
*pools* to ensure flexibility when it comes to current and emerging
needs.

## Developmental Linkages

The fourth dimension of a succession system is its developmental
linkages. In other words, the system identifies how positions are
tied to development along with the bosses overseeing these positions. It is critical that jobs identified for succession have specific
opportunities and characteristics related to development. If a position is for a director level job for marketing in Shanghai, then
what are the developmental opportunities that might lead up to
that job? Stretch assignments that provide tough challenges are
also highlighted in terms of specific jobs. An effective succession
system identifies shortages or gaps in the types of developmental
experiences and jobs and is constantly working to increase the
number of those.

Best practice companies typically employ a wide range of developmental activities to engage leaders and extend their capabilities. While these companies believe that job assignments are the
most significant developmental activity, many offer mentoring,

coaching, and action learning along with educational programs to complement learning related to a specific job.

## Assessors

The individuals who evaluate subordinates, determine who are "high potentials," and decide who gets promoted into what positions are major stakeholders in any succession system. Multiple levels of assessors need to be involved. It's not just an individual's boss who participates in the review, but also the boss's boss and peers with a cross-functional perspective. Increasingly, subordinates and external or internal customers are involved in the assessment process—often through 360-degree feedback tools. These assessments also include developmental dialogues with the individual regarding her or his future career interests and goals and the constraints she foresees. Participants should receive information about suggested activities for further growth. This information is complemented by individual development and career plans, so that all participants are forced to do reflective work on their developmental needs. All of this is supplemented with feedback, such as 360-degree feedback and coaching on the manager's overall effectiveness in a particular job and her overall readiness to move to the next assignment.

## Tracking

Tracking in the ideal system monitors progress and turnover. It records and analyzes exits of individuals who are talented and gaps at certain key levels and jobs, particularly linchpin jobs. Two types of data are traditionally collected: *quantitative* data, in terms of statistics of turnover and placement rates, and *qualitative* data, which analyzes individuals who are leaving, common problems that participants face in terms of their development and career progress, and dilemmas in using the succession system. Ideally, the tracking system also highlights the gap between planned assignments and actual assignments. This assessment enables top management to see whether or not the system is actually working according to the principles that guide it.

The use of technology for tracking in succession management varies widely within the best practice organizations. Yet, Web-based systems seem to offer great potential for worldwide access and large-scale integration of data. For instance, Dell has moved from more extensive, global software applications to a much simpler MS Excel workbook to organize data. Sonoco moved to integrate four commercial applications (PeopleSoft, HRCharter, Lotus Notes, and ExecuTRACK) into a seamless system that can be globally accessed and updated daily. The tracking watchwords are easy, accessible, and in an understandable format.

## Metrics

Finally, to tell whether the system is working, there are two types of metrics: *individual* metrics, which rate the individual candidate on performance versus perceived potential, and overall *system* metrics, which highlight the number of openings that are successfully filled internally by the succession system. These reports highlight the number of individuals who are selected on the list of high potentials and who ultimately obtain jobs related to a targeted development assignment.

There are also important metrics on diversity and cross-functional assignments that show how the organization is fulfilling key goals involving underrepresented segments of the workforce and general management development through multiple functional assignments. There should also be tracking systems and metrics that allow sponsors and owners to determine whether or not the succession system is working effectively to develop an adequate supply of leadership talent. For example, firms such as Dow and Lilly measure the portion of key jobs that are filled by insider versus outsider candidates. They believe that going outside on a regular basis for key people indicates that succession management is not working properly. Conversely, if all openings are filled by internal candidates, perhaps the company should worry about not getting enough new thinking into the ranks.

## Our Purpose

This book is designed to inspire companies to take what have been historically bureaucratic systems and turn them into powerful developmental tools. Our aim is to help the designers and users of succession planning tools understand how these systems—when supplemented with other leadership developmental activities—can be harnessed as dynamic tools for growing the next generation of leadership talent.

## Notes

1 Morgan McCall, *Lessons of Experience: How Successful Executives Develop on the Job* (New York: Free Press, 1988).
2 Ed Michaels, Helen Handfield-Jones, Beth Axelrod, *The War for Talent* (Boston: Harvard Business School Press, 2001).

# Chapter Two

# WHO SHOULD "OWN" SUCCESSION MANAGEMENT?

Historically, the human resources function has been the champion of succession planning. With its focus on employees and their development, this function is the natural owner of the succession management process. But to have sole responsibility is a mistake. Rather, the effectiveness of any succession system depends on a much broader set of owners and sponsors.

The most outspoken and committed "owner" must be the organization's CEO. This individual's willingness to champion a rigorous succession process sends a powerful signal throughout the organization that the firm is dedicated to developing and retain-

23

ing talent. The CEO's commitment also signals that the internal development of leadership capability is a priority and of strategic concern for the firm. At the same time, the CEO must engage his executive team as co-owners of succession management. This ensures a cascading effect with the individual executives holding their unit and functional managers accountable for the effective implementation of the process. As importantly, their emphasis on the development of their own subordinates models, for the rest of the organization, the attitudes and actions they are attempting to cultivate with a succession program.

When Ken Lewis took over as chairman and CEO at Bank of America in 1999, he immediately set forth on the journey of making the bank one of the world's most admired growth companies. Among the first actions he took was to instill in his direct reports and key leaders a mindset that "talent really matters." Accordingly, he decided to institutionalize organizational and talent reviews of his top talent within the businesses. During two-hour review sessions, Lewis probes to determine if each of the business units and its senior executive has:

- ❏ A grasp of the organizational capabilities it needs to win over the next twenty-four to thirty-six months

- ❏ Plans for developing those capabilities

- ❏ A succession strategy for filling key positions in these businesses

Additionally, these sessions are used to make decisions regarding the critical leadership talent moves over the next twelve to eighteen months needed to position the business unit for growth. In the quarterly business performance reviews he conducts with his direct reports, Mr. Lewis holds his executives accountable for commitments made in the annual talent reviews.

Once Lewis had established this talent review process as a critical routine for managing the corporation and completed the first year's meetings, he felt that it was imperative that all leaders be assessed against common leadership characteristics. Consequently, he commissioned the development of a new leadership model that defined those competencies as well as the derailers that would enable or inhibit success among senior leaders at Bank of America. These competences had to facilitate the strategic shift of the corporation from a reliance on growth by acquisitions to more organic growth. In the end, the model speaks Lewis's language—the type of leadership he expects and foresees as necessary to sustain growth into Bank of America's future.

Beyond the CEO and the executive team, the corporate human resources function should be responsible for the tools and processes that enable successful succession planning. They must ensure that the system is simple and rigorous and provides reliable assessments. In addition, they must design and champion systems that provide uniform standards for the entire organization while simultaneously reinventing the system to reflect evolving needs.

The final set of "owners" or sponsors are the business or functional unit heads and their human resources teams who are ultimately responsible for the deliverables of succession management. Senior unit and functional managers must not see the process as one that is forced on them or as one that is time consuming and bureaucratic. Rather, they must feel that the system serves their own needs for talented managers. In this chapter, we explore these various owners and describe the forms their ownership roles must take to ensure succession planning that provides a deep and capable bench of talent.

# The Most Critical Owner and Champion: The CEO and the Senior Team

For any organization that wishes to engage in truly effective succession planning, senior-level commitment is absolutely essential. We would also argue that verbal support from the top is not enough. Rather the CEO and her executive team must be enthusiastic champions. They must believe deeply that talent provides a competitive advantage that directly impacts organizational performance. They must also hold their direct reports accountable for ensuring that the "system" is a rigorous and reliable one—in other words, that talent is retained and developed and that talent gaps are quickly recognized and actions taken to address them. Moreover, they must fundamentally believe that talent is a corporate-wide resource, not the property of a particular function or division. This approach was best exemplified by General Electric under Jack Welch's tenure. Welch was famous for his comment to his business heads about the company's top 500 executives: "I own the people. You just rent them." Finally, they must focus more of their attention on the development or preparation side of the talent equation, rather than simply on the metrics and inventory side.

Without this level of critical support by the very top, succession management can end up a more mechanical process with "hit or miss" results. Sensing that succession planning is simply a tangential activity, division executives can vary widely in their commitments to the development of their subordinates. Operating groups and functions can hide or hoard their talent by manipulating their assessments. Limited attention will be given to genuine developmental assignments. Our own findings in the APQC study powerfully confirm the necessity of this commitment from the very top. The best practice organizations we studied had senior management more involved in succession planning than in the sponsor organizations (see Figure 2-1). Examples of senior level buy-in at the best-practice organizations follow.

For example, Sonoco's executive committee, composed of eight members including the CEO, the vice president of HR, the CFO, and top group vice presidents, meets annually for an entire week to discuss succession planning. The willingness of the top team to invest so much time attests to the commitment that senior leaders have to succession planning. The executive committee review process involves an in-depth examination of each division's management talent. These discussions are focused on the performance, potential for promotion, and placement of individual managers within a specific division. The executive committee is able to question the decisions taken by the division senior management teams. These meetings are conducted in open forum format, and executives may pose any question they wish. The goal of this week-long meeting is to approve the placement of specific

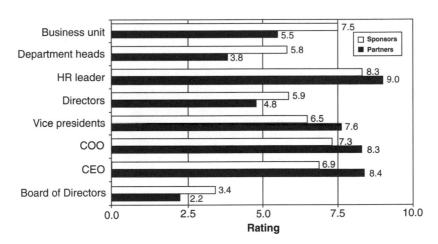

Figure 2-1. Level of involvement of the following leaders as it relates to the Succession Management process (1 being limited involvement, 10 being extensive involvement).

individuals within the company's performance/promotion status matrix. The corporate HR team facilitates the discussions and records decisions and discussions.

At PanCanadian, president and CEO David Tuer was the main driver for the petroleum company's first succession management initiative. He assigned human resources to steward the process, established a Centre of Excellence, and mandated attendance at the first People Conference. The Centre of Excellence (COE) designed, integrated, and managed data for succession management and reported directly into corporate HR. At the corporate level, a committee of vice presidents oversaw the day-to-day work of succession management. At the business level, general managers managed the process by completing succession management analyses, taking action to address issues, and participating in the People Conference. This conference was a forum to discuss current and future organizational requirements for leadership talent across the organization.

Without the support and commitment of top management, it is almost impossible to operate an effective succession planning process. Executive level buy-in is critical for the financial support and to affirm genuine commitment to the process for all employees. One of the greatest advantages of top level support, however, is that it ensures a much tighter link to the organization's overall business strategy and to the corporate values. Like every other aspect of a successful organization, succession management has to facilitate, rather than hinder, the achievement of the corporate goals. For example, Dell Computer requires its succession planning process to align the growth of the leadership pool with the plans for the organization's growth. Dell's process includes a review of leadership needs across the firm; review of existing leadership talent; identification of gaps between needs and talent; development of plans to close those gaps; executive review (the office of the chairman (OOC) presentation); and ongoing development, movement, and measurement of leadership talent.

At Eli Lilly and Company, the chief executive officer holds day-long annual reviews with function heads. There are four goals for the meeting:

1. Demonstrate senior leadership commitment to talent identification and development.

2. Ensure that area "people objectives" are aligned with corporate and area business objectives.

3. Assess the organization—determine the strength of the leadership team and the talent pipeline, understand and drive improvements in the diversity of the current and potential management team, and lastly review key position succession plans.

4. In-depth review of key individuals and their development plans.

At PanCanadian, a human resources strategy was combined with the corporate competitive strategy to achieve its long-term business goals more successfully. This people strategy outlined the corporate approach to employee management and cultural requirements in direct connection to the company's overall business plan. Developed and refreshed annually, this people strategy employed the organization's business strategy as a base to understand cultural requirements, such as agility and innovation. As shown in Figure 2-2, the strategy identified ways to attract and retain people, in significant part through development and succession management.

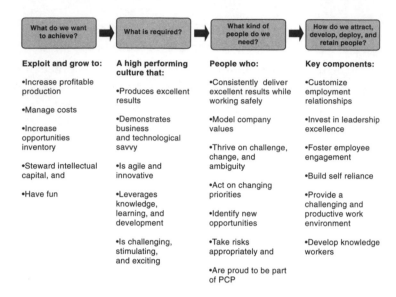

Figure 2-2. PanCanadian's 2001–2003 people strategy.

By linking succession planning with the overall business strategy, best practice organizations cement the position of succession planning as an integral and vital process. From such an integral position, succession planning gains a position of greater impact over the organization's long-term goals and objectives. Again, this outcome is more likely to occur when CEOs and their top team are actively involved in the process and serve as outspoken champions.

But it is not realistic or desirable for CEOs to be solely responsible for the development of talent and leadership. Not only do they have little expertise in developing talent, but they are usually exposed only to those with the highest potential and have extremely limited knowledge of up-and-coming junior-level leaders. Moreover, the demands on the typical CEO make it difficult for the top person to devote enough time to this single issue. Other players or "owners" are needed.

# Human Resources: The Process Owners

In our findings, senior human resources leaders play the most extensive role in owning the succession process, followed by the
CEO and COO in partnership with the business units. The best
practice partners in the APQC project were clear on the critical
role of human resources in making the *processes* behind succession
management work. They also recognized the pivotal role of integrating their overall leadership development process (typically an
HR responsibility) into the structure of the succession management processes. As indicated in Figure 2-1, each of the partner
organizations housed their succession planning process within
HR. In contrast, nearly 20 percent of the sponsor group had a
separate function to manage and align the succession planning
process. We believe that alignment of succession planning and
leadership development is achieved far more easily when these
activities report to a common organizational entity—in this case,
the corporate HR function. In addition, those in charge of succession planning activities should report directly to the most senior
HR executive. If succession is indeed a top corporate priority, its
status in the hierarchy needs to reflect it.

With the focus of the new generation of succession systems
on development, the integration of leadership development and
succession is a particularly critical task. In a typical global company, there are usually regional heads for its dispersed operations,
senior managers who oversee the company's multiple lines of business, and executives from the functional areas embedded within
the business lines, geographical organizations, and corporate center. Given such complexity, it is easy to find multiple centers for
leadership-development activities, each with a different owner

but lacking any overall sense of coherence. If succession management is housed in a separate function or is in limited contact with these development efforts, then the succession process may be seriously hampered in its ability to link plans to developmental activities and may also produce greatly divergent results. This reporting relationship is particularly important in highly decentralized firms, where it is not uncommon to have HR specialists in each business unit running leadership-development initiatives suited to that unit's specific needs. These are always coordinated with the company's succession strategy as a whole.

For example, at Bank of America, each business unit has a senior HR generalist and leadership development executive assigned to it, but these individuals report directly to the corporate personnel function in order to ensure an enterprise-view or total corporation perspective of issues, needs, talent, and succession. It is these business partners who help develop, at the business unit level, the talent management and development processes that support the bank's overall succession planning actions and decisions. It is at this level, where the talent management and review processes are integrated into the quarterly, if not monthly, management routines (performance reviews, talent calibration sessions, staff meetings, staffing), that the business unit's leadership teams drive their business' growth.

At Dell Computer, the office of the chairman (OOC) is the champion and final audience for the succession management process. This office includes the CEO and two COOs. Annually, each business unit leader presents his succession plans and leadership development objectives to the OOC. At quarterly meetings, the OOC discusses possible transfers among the business units with individual business heads. While business unit leaders are ultimately accountable for developing the leadership potential within their units, they rely on customized tools and processes provided by corporate human resources (the executive and organization development group). This HR group consists of six individuals responsible for designing and rolling out leadership development processes throughout the company. One individual within that group primarily handles the succession management process and tools. Human resources groups within each business unit support and are integrated into the succession and leadership development processes.

Dow Chemical's executive management team, which consists of the CEO and fourteen direct reports, actively manages three groups:

1. The seventy roles in the organization that are considered "corporate critical." These are global roles that will not change significantly because of an incumbent and the roles are absolutely critical to the company's success. The group actively manages the succession plan for each of those roles.

2. The top 250 roles, which are referred to as the "Global Leadership" job family. The executive management group annually evaluates the incumbents of those roles and actively manages all activities associated with the roles (placement, development, and compensation).

3. The list of 800 to 900 future leaders who are being developed by the businesses and functions as the eventual pool to feed the succession planning process and fill critical functional roles.

This entire focus is led jointly by the CEO, the head of HR, and the leader of Workforce Planning, who serves as the facilitator of the process. The Corporate Operating Board, which in-

cludes the CEO and his fourteen direct reports, oversees Dow's
succession management process from the executive level by reviewing the professional development of the future leaders from
the previous year and assessing nominees for the upcoming year's
development investments. Thus, the Corporate Operating Board
"owns" the process, and the HR business partners and the Workforce Planning Strategic Center work together to facilitate it.
Within the corporate HR department, the global director of
workforce planning is the focal point for succession management.
An internal HR design team benchmarks, upgrades, and improves
the process.

Eli Lilly and Company's CEO and its vice president of human
resources drive its succession management process. The succession management team resides within the corporate human resources department and owns the process that manages the
organization's talent. The succession management team develops
the tools that insure consistency of information gathered by providing templates, definitions, and tools that result in a single
*corporate-wide* database of employee information. Through a comprehensive intranet site, Lilly's succession management team facilitates professional development planning, identifies associate
potential, formulates succession metrics, and manages employee
data for the entire firm.

Returning to Bank of America, the head of Personnel (equal
to the vice president of human resources) and the CEO drive
its succession management process. The Executive Development
function within the corporate human resources department is responsible for designing, developing, and then educating senior operating leaders on the use of the talent review tools and processes
to drive the level of discussion and decisions needed (see Figure
2-3). It is also Executive Development that has responsibility for
the consistency of the background data gathered by providing

**Key Talent:**
- Leaders who EXCEED performance expectations against EITHER the "what" and the "how" AND ARE AT LEAST MEETS on the other scale.

- Key talent leaders to focus on/invest in for talent planning purposes include: (1) "**HiPos**", and (2) "**HiPros**" (those who are not high potential but critical to retain because of performance, skills, and expertise).

**Top-Grading Opportunities:**
- Leaders who are not meeting "what" performance expectations (i.e., not delivering results). Immediate 60–90 day action plans for improvement must be in place.

**Leadership Issues:**
- Leaders who are delivering results but are not demonstrating leadership behaviors required for success. Immediate coaching and improvement plans are required. If leadership behaviors don't improve, these individuals represent future top grade opportunities.

Performance Results,
**"The What"**

Exceeds Expectations

Meets Expectations

Does Not Meet Expectations

P. Chin ☆
W. Lewin (WP)

F. Ravaux ☆

E. Sanchez (E)

**Key Talent**

H. Smith (I)

**Top-Grading Opportunities**

**Leadership Issues**

Does Not Meet Expectations | Meets Expectations | Exceeds Expectations

Leadership Behaviors,
**"The How"**

**Potential:**
☆ High Potential
**E** Expandable
**WP** Well Placed
**I** Issue

Note: not actual names.

Figure 2-3. Performance and Potential Summary for Bank of America Talent Reviews—Example.

common sets of templates, definitions, and tools that result in a single *corporate-wide* talent management database of key leader information. While there is a small corporate entity accountable for defining the bank's overall succession planning process and designing the supporting tools and frameworks for executing it, there are also Leadership Development partners (reporting to corporate HR) assigned to each line of business. These partners are ultimately accountable for bringing the *corporate* processes to life in a way that makes the best sense for their business unit but within the overall context and requirements of the entire enterprise. These Leadership Development partners are the ones who facilitate the talent management decisions within the individual business units and then work with these units' senior leaders to design the right structures to enable the right talent moves, as well as manage and track commitments made around talent management.

## Ownership Below the Executive Level: The Implementers

In the early days of succession planning, most systems were concerned only with the senior-most talent. There was little emphasis on even general management positions, let alone middle management. As the emphasis has shifted from a "replacement" process to a developmental one, however, more and more succession processes reach deeper into the organization. While top-level buy-in is critical in getting a succession management system up and running, the effective implementation of these processes depends in large part on management below the executive level. After all, it is spotting emerging talent, performing the actual talent assessments, and identifying developmental opportunities.

As shown in Figure 2-4, 80 percent of best practice partners engage in succession management activities below the executive level. These additional levels include general managers, directors, and managers. Of the sponsor group, 67 percent conduct succession planning below the executive level for general managers, directors, and managers. Examples of the ways in which the best practice organizations manage such succession planning are described below (see Figure 2-4).

Sonoco addresses succession planning at the plant manager, area manager, and general manager levels. Three separate group level meetings are held to address succession planning with these managers. In all three meetings, five key principles guide decision making:

*Principle 1—"Build from the bottom up."* The goal is to start at the bottom of the organization with the plant managers and move up through the area managers to the general managers. The data builds on itself, which is especially helpful when examining key issues across the organization.

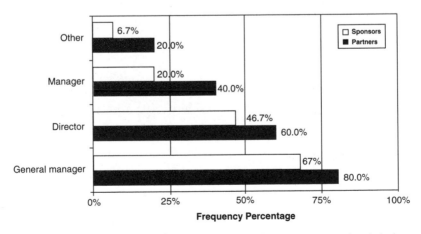

Figure 2-4. Succession Management activities for organization levels below the executive level.

*Principle 2—"Involve those who are closest."* The meetings involve the people who are closest to the individuals being evaluated—those who observe the individual begin evaluated on a daily basis. Often it is the individual's supervisor who is involved in these discussions and in the actual succession decisions.

*Principle 3—"Use the performance data."* Decisions should be taken using the performance management documents of those being evaluated. Other data should be examined as well, including employee profiles, education, and work history, as well as interactions and observations of the management team regarding the individual.

*Principle 4—"Use consensus decision making."* The decision-making process should involve more than just the supervisor and should arrive at a well deliberated consensus.

*Principle 5—"Time investment is a requirement."* Many discussions are required, and this activity is not necessarily a linear, sequential process. It requires a significant commitment of time for the human resources specialists and line executives. Nevertheless, the system should be designed for efficiency and to provide reasonable returns on the time investment.

For each Sonoco division, succession planning begins with the plant managers. The vice president and area managers meet offsite for a full day with the division's HR manager to assess the plant managers' performance and potential for promotion. This group uses the consensus process to identify where each one of the company's 40 plant managers falls on the performance or promotability matrix.

As each person is discussed, the group reviews the performance management document, as well as her competencies, completed objectives for the year, and personal development plans. The prior year's succession planning data is also incorporated, so that the group can see if the individual has changed positions on the performance matrix, and if so, why.

At the plant manager level, the purpose of the meeting is to identify performance or promotability factors, not successors. Therefore, the results are a *pool* of potential successors rather than select individuals identified as successors.

The outcome of these discussions is a clearer understanding of total group strength. Everyone at the plant manager level is plotted on the matrix, and the group identifies areas of strength and weakness (e.g., the division is weak at the top category or has too many people at the top). Based on its findings, the group may also formulate plans for employee development.

Six layers of the matrix are reviewed. The top two layers are the direct reports to the division general managers and the next level down of direct reports (i.e., successor candidates). The remaining four cuts include a matrix on regional manufacturing managers, regional sales managers, sales people below the manager level, and plant or location managers. Each level is plotted on a separate matrix. Corporate HR asks each division to produce these six matrices and bring them with the other review materials. Corporate HR then communicates the results of the meetings to the divisions. The divisions are reminded to focus on individuals in the high and low potential boxes of the matrix, to look at the key issues, and to act on them. A similar process is then conducted for area managers and general managers.

Dow Chemical, on the other hand, does not conduct formal succession planning for positions below the top 900 roles that are considered in the executive group and therefore seen as a corporate asset. Instead, job openings for these positions are posted online on the Job Announcement System (JAS), which creates open access for employees to most jobs. JAS lets employees take control of their own careers, because employees can simply visit the Web site and view available positions globally in thirteen languages.

Talented candidates for higher-level positions (that fall between the scope of the Job Announcement System and the Corporate Operating Board's full review of the top 250 positions) are generated by the business functions through what is called the "Future Leader" (or high potential) process. These candidates are then analyzed in the annual people reviews. At people reviews, the Corporate Operating Board reviews the professional development of the Future Leaders from the previous year and nominees for the upcoming year's development investments.

The four stages of professional development at Dow are called *acquiring, applying, leveraging,* and *visioning.* In the *acquiring* stage, employees are expected to obtain the competencies and experiences required to become fully qualified in their profession, for example as an accountant, research scientist, or production engineer. Employees cannot spend their careers at the *acquiring* stage. They must progress at least to the *applying* stage. The *applying* stage expects the employee to apply these professional competencies and experiences to achieving the business strategy. Most employees spend their career at this stage. In the *leveraging* stage, the employee is highly experienced and is now expected to leverage her competencies and experience across businesses and/or countries on a global basis. Approximately 20 percent of the employees progress to this stage.

The *vision* stage is treated more as a job/role level than a development stage. These are roles where the future direction of the country, function, or business are determined or lead. Less than 7 percent of the leadership roles are in this stage. The Corporate Operating Board discusses each future leader with regard to these stages. Then, the functional leaders on the Corporate Operating Board and their staffs fill their higher-level jobs. Though succession planning takes place for most of these roles, the process is not monitored at a corporate level, but, rather within the functional leadership teams.

Dell Computer identifies high-potential talent at the corporate level (called "Global Corporate Talent") and at the business unit level (called "functional high-potentials"). Anyone specified as Global Corporate Talent is also profiled and reviewed for the OOC. The Global Corporate Talent pool consists of individuals with the capability to run significant portions of a function or business, i.e., a person who can leverage skills and experience on a global basis. Dell invests a significant amount of resources and senior management time on this Global Corporate Talent pool, which is made up of fewer than 100 individuals in the company. Dell business units also have functional high-potential programs that identify talent deeper within their organizations. The functional high potentials are generally not reviewed in the OOC presentations.

At Bank of America, the succession planning process is driven top down and bottom up. It is at the individual/functional unit level where the beginning of the process starts, rolling up to the meetings that occur with the CEO. The CEO reviews and *personally* puts his stamp of approval on the decisions surrounding the top 100 jobs. Lewis and his executive team oversee the top 250 jobs. The lines of business then have responsibility for their own talent. In each business line, they have the ability to determine how deep they take the succession process, depending on the needs and objectives of their business. Some choose to review two levels below the line's senior leader. Others might choose three or four levels deep. Ultimately, it is the senior leader of each line of business who owns the talent decisions. They are held accountable for ensuring that they have made the correct calibration/ assessment of key talent to help their unit's success. It is at this level where true accountability for decisions, actions, and commitments is tracked and monitored. Then, the senior most leaders are held accountable for ensuring that the right players are in the right jobs. So accountability for succession rests largely in the hands of senior line managers.

# Conclusion

Best practice organizations work to solidify the position of succession planning as an activity vital to the organization's long-term success. They begin with strong champions at the very top. The CEO and her senior team ensure that talent retention and development are seen as one of the corporation's highest priorities. Through their time and commitment to the succession process, they encourage managers throughout the organization to take the process seriously. In best practice organizations, the human resources group is responsible for the tools and processes that make successful succession planning a reality and continually looks for ways to make the process simpler, yet more rigorous. Business or line units are responsible for the deliverables—in other words, for ensuring that assessments are performed thoroughly and accurately, that talent gets the opportunities it needs for development, and that gaps in talent are quickly identified and resolved. It is through this "chain" of committed owners that succession planning becomes the organization's most powerful tool for identifying, retaining, and developing leadership talent.

One fascinating finding from our study was that sponsor organizations actually spent more hours on the succession planning process than partner organizations did. They had a greater number of meetings and spent more hours per meeting at all levels. Based on these findings, we could infer that the succession management process at best practice organizations must be considered more efficient and effective than the process at sponsor organizations. The exemplars have developed systems that require less investment of time, and this efficiency leads to greater utilization by line executives.

# Chapter Three

# DEFINING AND IDENTIFYING TALENT

At the foundation of succession management is the definition and identification of talent—what it looks like, who has it, who needs to develop it, and how it can best be developed. The challenge, however, is defining what is meant by the term "talent" in light of the needs of the organization and how to achieve accurate assessments of it. Historically, performance outcomes were the simplest way to determine who had "talent" and who did not. The thinking was simple: those with the greatest current performance must be our most talented leaders. But experience has shown that this line of thinking is often inaccurate. Organizations have learned again that individuals with high performance outcomes

45

at one level do not always repeat that high performance at the next level. The demands of positions ahead may be so different that one's current skill set proves inadequate. Weaknesses or talent gaps that are less harmful at junior levels become more pronounced at senior ones. Strengths that ensured success early in one's career can prove to be insufficient or, even worse, can become liabilities in future roles. As a result, interest has grown in assessing a person's "potential" for advancement or—more accurately—potential for "development."

In addition, leadership today is considered one of the most important capabilities for senior managers. With this in mind, more and more organizations have incorporated leadership competencies into their assessments. These competencies in turn form the basis both for professional development (discussed in this chapter) and for performance management (discussed in Chapters 4 and 5). In essence, they set the standards for leadership and more often reflect the expectations of the top executives. In describing the competency model devised at Bank of America, Brian Fishel, senior vice president of executive recruiting and development, commented, "The language and feel of our leadership competency model is very much that of our CEO. His expectations pervade—about the performance and results we expect, about how to deliver them, about the need to constantly 'raise the bar' on ourselves because the customers we serve demand that we deliver to ever higher standards, and about the derailing behaviors that will cause leaders to fail at Bank of America." The APQC study found that, in almost every case, alignment between competency models, corporate performance objectives, and employees was a key characteristic of effectiveness with succession management processes.

As we illustrate in this chapter, once performance expectations and competency models are in place, best practice corporations use a variety of identification tools to achieve alignment. Many companies employ these tools not only to identify individual employees, but also to create talent pools from which employees can be drawn when positions open. Using simple graphic matrices, individuals are assessed along the dimensions of current performance as well as their potential, with ratings of low, medium, and high readiness for promotion. Performance criteria typically include achievement of current goals and ongoing demonstration of values and leadership competencies, while potential is based on the individual's ability to successfully lead at the next level.

The most effective succession processes simultaneously identify the appropriate developmental opportunity for the individual if they are ready for promotion. With rigorous assessments, succession management systems then become powerful development tools—identifying those who are ready for the next assignment and which assignments can best serve their developmental needs. When viewed across levels of the organization, the succession process can also provide equally powerful insights into what types of developmental assignments are currently in short supply, what types of assignments are needed for future demands, and where the gaps or shortages of talent are.

# Competency Models: The Benchmarks for Succession

As succession systems have grown more sophisticated, they have moved away from a complete reliance on the individual's current performance—in other words, on simply "making their numbers." As we mentioned in the beginning of this chapter, the better systems now incorporate assessments of the individual's leadership capabilities, adherence to the organization's values, and capacity for development and learning in addition to pure performance outcomes. To make these kinds of assessments, succession planning systems rely on competencies—these are the benchmarks against which talent is assessed and the needs for talent identified.

Competency models trace their origins back to the traditional "job description," which, in a rudimentary way, helped management identify the appropriate employee for each position while simultaneously informing employees (or potential employees) about the skill sets that were prerequisites for the position. The job description also formed the basis for employee evaluations.

As computer and other technical skills began to grow in importance during the second half of the last century, human resources departments were faced for the first time with hiring people with skill sets that neither they nor upper management understood. In response, the human resource (HR) function began to develop lists of competencies necessary for success in technical positions. Harvard psychology professor David McClelland drew attention to the value of competences in the early 1970s. In an article entitled "Testing for Competence Rather Than 'Intelligence,'" McClelland raised the issue of why intelligence tests were poor predictors of job success.[1] He argued that another set of factors—competences—were better at explaining success. It was, however, the publication of a book in 1982 entitled *The Competent Manager* by a protégé of McClelland's, Richard Boyatzis, that sparked greater interest in competency modeling. Boyatzis defined a competency as "an underlying characteristic of a person—a motive, trait, skill, aspect of one's self image or social role, or a body of knowledge which he or she uses."[2]

Today, we associate the term "competencies" with the behaviors and skills that are necessary for success in a particular role. By the late 1980s, companies began to develop "competency models" for the selection and assessment of their management positions. As interest in leadership and leadership development grew in the 1990s, competency models received a further boost. After all, organizations needed clear definitions of what they wanted in leadership behavior. In recent years, corporate values and learning capability, as well as derailment behaviors (such as arrogance or lack of integrity; behaviors that cause high potential managers to fall off the "high potential list" or simply to fail), have been added into the competency mix as well.

The enormous popularity of developmental tools such as 360-degree feedback finally cemented the position of competency models as essential to the development and assessment field. A study conducted during the U.S. Leadership Development Conference in June 2001 found that competency modeling was used by almost 75 percent of all companies as a tool for leadership development.[3] The same study showed that 69 percent of the development initiatives of mid-level managers were using competency models as a basis for developing training initiatives. A study conducted by Arthur Andersen Worldwide also found that the majority of companies had applied competency models in the area of training and development.[4] In the APQC study, all of the best practice companies used competency models in all phases of the succession management process.

Companies employing competency models as the foundation of their succession management process have found that they provide a variety of benefits. Specifically, competency models:

❑ Convey clear expectations for roles and for levels of performance

❑ Provide more valid and uniform corporate planning data

❑ Link development activities to organizational goals

❑ Motivate employees to improve by providing specific guidelines for professional development

❑ Protect the morale of both supervisors and subordinates by quantifying performance management

❑ Streamline HR activities

❑ Provide a common framework and language for discussing how to implement and communicate key talent and leadership development strategies

❑ Help set expectations for current senior leaders and/or serve as development targets for those in the organization who aspire to become a senior leader in the future

While many of the earlier competency models had relatively long lists of competencies, there has been a trend toward simplifying the number of dimensions to a set of "core" competences. This notion of "core competencies" derives from the work of Gary Hamel and C. K. Prahalad, who introduced the concept to the business vocabulary in an award winning *Harvard Business Review* article.[5] While their concept dealt with the utilization of unique *organizational* capabilities that provided strategic advantage, the term has since been applied to those basic (or core) *personal behaviors* associated with successful leaders in a particular organization. Thus, we found that our best practice organizations begin with a *core* set of competencies—behaviors, mindsets, and values that they believe should be shared company-wide. Each competency then has a set of tangible descriptors that illustrate that particular competency "in action." The APQC study found that most best practice organizations use these core competencies to evaluate employees on an individual or team basis and to identify and evaluate employees' leadership potential. These succession management competencies are likewise aligned with corporate goals.

In addition, all best practice organizations in the APQC study reported that they use succession management competencies in other processes such as performance management, training and development, and 360-degree feedback. They employ the succession management, competencies as criteria for promotion, compensation, mentoring, and recruiting more frequently than our control group organizations. In doing so, they ensure that the competencies are reinforced at every opportunity. A benefit of the consistent use of an identified set of competencies is integration across multiple HR systems. This integration is critical to achieving the simplicity that many organizations desire. Figure 3-1 contrasts the linkage of these other processes to succession management competencies in both best practice organizations (black lines) and the control group (white lines).

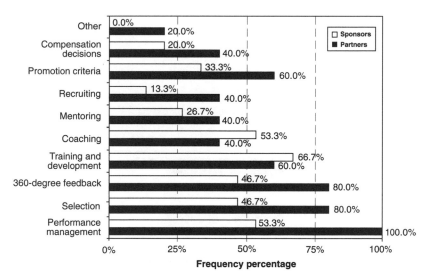

Figure 3-1. Linkage of HR processes to Succession Management competencies.

The best practice organizations use fewer of these core competencies in their models than do the control group organizations. Figure 3-2 compares the number of competencies used by the two groups in performance management, development activities, and selection and identification. There is a strong desire on the part of the best practice organizations to keep the succession process as simple as possible. A smaller list of core competences ensures a less complicated process and provides greater clarity around the essential behaviors and activities that are and will be rewarded by the organization.

## Sample Competency Models in Best Practice Organizations

Dell Computer's core competency model is the backbone for all of the company's succession and leadership activities. The chosen competencies are those associated with the firm's strongest per-

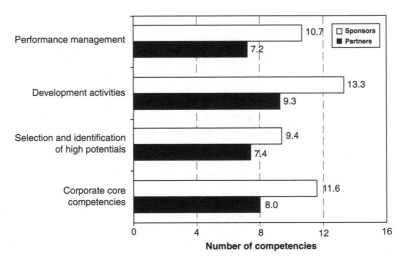

Figure 3-2. How many competencies do you use for the following?

forming leaders across the business units and specific functions and are identified as core to their success. The model was created using an analysis of 360-degree feedback data and performance appraisals of high and low performers, derailment studies, strategic organizational requirements, and benchmarking data. Dell employees are assessed against the following five core competencies for entry-level leadership positions:

1. Functional technical skills

2. Integrity and trust

3. Intellectual horsepower

4. Business acumen

5. Command skills

Additionally, the following nine competencies were identified as success factors for Dell leaders:

1. Priority setting

2. Problem solving

3. Drive for results

4. Building effective teams

5. Developing direct reports

6. Customer focus

7. Organization agility

8. Learning on the fly

9. Dealing with ambiguity

Dow has eight corporate-wide and global competencies:

1. Initiative

2. Innovation

3. Interpersonal effectiveness

4. Leadership

5. Learning

6. Market focus

7. Teamwork

8. Value creation

In addition to these eight, each Dow function uses a second set of competencies that are function specific. In other words, each of its global functions has a separate set of competencies, which are used in hiring, evaluating, and compensating employees. For example, the Accounting function has decided on four function-specific competencies:

1. Information technology

2. Reporting and consulting

3. Technical knowledge

4. Work process discipline

In contrast, the Manufacturing function has chosen the following five function-specific competencies:

1. Information technology

2. Productivity focus

3. Responsible care (environment, health, and safety)

4. Technical capability

5. Work process discipline

Eli Lilly and Company utilizes seven leadership behaviors in its assessment of performance and potential:

1. Model the values

2. Create external focus

3. Anticipate change and prepare for the future

4. Implement with quality speed and value

5. Achieve results with people

6. Evaluate and act

7. Share key learnings

Similar to Dow, Lilly has developed additional sets of competencies that apply to a specific function and vary by specific management level.

PanCanadian's leadership competencies were developed using a combination of academic research, assessment of top performers, and strategic fit. The following PanCanadian leadership competencies were applicable to all management levels:

❑ Visionary

❑ Effective communication

❑ Decisiveness and follow-through

❑ Business acumen

❑ People/team management

❑ Innovation

❑ Change management

Because Bank of America was going through a critical transition, the organization recognized that its leaders would need to perform to a different set of expectations to succeed. Ken Lewis "commissioned" its executive development team to facilitate the development of a new senior leadership competency model illustrative of the new environment he was creating and, more importantly, which made transparent the competencies and behaviors that senior leaders would have to master in order for Bank of America to succeed, not just for today but over the next three to five years as well.

As Executive Development went about developing the bank's new leadership model, it conducted behavioral event interviews with the top eighty-eight executives from across various jobs to ensure that an enterprise view and applicability benchmarked other top growth companies' leadership requirements; companies researched included Allied Signal, General Electric, 3M, Honeywell, Coca-Cola, PepsiCo, Wells-Fargo, Citigroup, and UPS, to name a few outside firms consulted with that specialize in leadership competency models. In the end, it was determined that the final product had to be specific to Bank of America and speak its language of growth for the model to be most applicable, relevant, and used there. Hence, the final leadership model developed is highly tailored to the bank's needs.

At the Bank of America, there is a single leadership compe-

| I. Grow the Business | II. Lead People to Perform | III. Drive Execution | IV. Sustain Intensity and Optimism |
|---|---|---|---|
| A. Demonstrates deep and broad business acumen<br>1. Demonstrates deep/broad financial management and functional skills<br>2. Demonstrates a business perspective that is much broader than one function or unit<br>3. Cuts to the heart of complex business and financial issues<br>B. Creates competitive and innovative business plans<br>4. Creates competitive, innovative business plans that drive short- and long-term growth.<br>5. Challenges the status quo to grow the business<br>6. Focuses on growth opportunities and capital efficient investments<br>7. Reinvents the business<br>C. Builds customer/client-driven environment<br>8. Ensures the customer/client perspective is at forefront of all business decisions and initiatives<br>9. Invests time in customer/client-facing activities to understand their needs<br>10. Instills customer/client focus in all associates<br>D. Institutionalizes error-free quality processes<br>11. Champions and leverages six sigma tools to drive revenue, reduce costs, and add value<br>12. Holds all associates accountable for continuously improving processes<br>E. Excels at risk/reward trade-off<br>13. Thoroughly analyzes opportunities issues and then takes appropriate risks<br>14. Takes action to mitigate and minimize liabilities, while ensuring maximum returns | F. Aligns enterprise capabilities<br>15. Transcends silos to achieve greater enterprise results<br>16. Drives collaboration among individuals and groups<br>17. Leverages teams to drive performance<br>G. Recruits and grows great talent<br>18. Acts as a champion for diversity, creating an environment that values diverse backgrounds and perspectives<br>19. Is superb at selecting "A" players<br>20. Moves quickly to address mediocre/poor performers<br>21. Willingly takes risks on high potentials/high performers to stretch and develop them<br>H. Inspires commitment and followership<br>22. Paints a compelling picture of the future and connects it to individual associates<br>23. Creates positive energy in the face of challenges<br>24. Inspires others to follow his/her lead<br>I. Communicates crisply and candidly<br>25. Balances talking and listening to foster candid dialogue<br>26. Crisply gets his/her point across<br>27. Commands attention across multiple audiences | J. Instills management focus and discipline<br>28. Implements practices and processes that drive accountability<br>29. Translates strategies into specific goals, tactics, action plans, and deliverables<br>30. Keeps people focused<br>K. Builds partnerships to achieve swift adoption<br>31. Builds broad-based business relationships across the organization<br>32. Skillfully influences peers and colleagues to promote and sell ideas<br>33. Brings to surface and resolves conflict with minimal noise<br>L. Demonstrates sound judgment and acts with speed<br>34. Balances data, logic, and intuition in decision making<br>35. Deals effectively with concrete, tangible issues as well as abstract, conceptual matters<br>36. Makes timely decisions<br>37. Generates pragmatic, sensible, and simple solutions to complex problems<br>38. Moves quickly to eliminate roadblocks | M. Constantly raises the bar<br>39. Sets "stretch" performance standards for self and others<br>40. Creates the optimal tension for peak performance<br>41. Demonstrates low tolerance for mediocrity<br>42. Fosters high levels of accountability through fair, but hard-hitting performance management processes<br>N. Displays personal courage<br>43. Takes a stand on controversial and unpopular issues<br>44. Makes tough business and people decisions<br>O. Continuously learns and adapts<br>45. Is insightful about personal mistakes and failures: learns from them and moves on<br>46. Is a voracious learner |

| Live Our Values | | | |
|---|---|---|---|
| 47. Lives our company's values<br>48. Puts the interest of the bank ahead of his/her own agenda | | | |

Figure 3-3. Exhibit 1, Bank of America leadership competencies with behaviors.

tency model for the top four levels of the organization (approx. 10,000 associates—Figure 3-3 on the previous page).While each line of business has the opportunity to add one to three technical/functional competencies to the list as needed, the core enterprise-model is used to set performance expectations for the senior-most three levels and developmental benchmarks for the fourth level. It is built around five basic dimensions:

1. Growing the business

2. Leading people to perform

3. Driving execution

4. Sustaining intensity and optimism

5. Living our company values

In addition, there is a set of derailing competences (Figure 3-4).

Best practice organizations have learned that competency models are most effective when they (1) include a small number of competencies, (2) define specific behaviors associated with each, and (3) employ a single set of competences for assessment. In the past, Sonoco, Lilly, and Dow had different sets of competencies for different levels of the organization, as well as separate competencies for functions such as hiring, development, and compensation. Each of these companies has since developed one core set of competencies and has carefully defined the desired behaviors for each. Universal competencies ensure greater consistency and better calibration in assessments across the enterprise.

## Identification Tools

The best practice organizations use a variety of tools and techniques for identifying future talent and leadership potential. In

| Failing to Deliver Results | Betraying Trust | Resisting Change | Being Exclusive vs. Inclusive | Failing to Take a Stand | Over Leading and Under Managing |
|---|---|---|---|---|---|
| 1. Fails to hold self and others accountable for results<br><br>2. Overpromises and underdelivers | 3. Says one thing and does another<br><br>4. Makes excuses or blames others<br><br>5. Shades, manages, withholds information to promote his/her personal or functional agenda | 6. Has trouble with adapting to new plans, programs, or priorities | 7. Fails to understand and take into account others' perspectives<br><br>8. Devalues the opinions and suggestions of others<br><br>9. Fails to engage others with different perspectives or skills than him/herself. | 10. Is indecisive<br><br>11. Stays on the fence on tough issues; won't weigh in until boss weighs in | 12. Lets details fall through the cracks<br><br>13. Fails to get involved with the day-to-day workings of the business unit |

Figure 3-4. Exhibit 2, Bank of America leadership model derailers.

most cases, the identification process is facilitated by dedicated members of the human resources organization working in partnership with the executives doing the actual assessments. Examples of tools used by the best practice partners in the APQC study are reviewed below. They include Lilly's "Talent ID Tool" and Sonoco's Performance/Promotability Matrix. Other tools used are performance management results and multi-rater feedback. In particular, 360-degree feedback data is now an essential source of information for succession assessments. This tool ensures that the multiple views of bosses, subordinates, and peers are not only included in the assessment process but also compared across a set of the identical competency dimensions. Given the critical role that subordinates play in determining whether one possesses leadership capabilities or not, this group of individuals has become an essential source for feedback. As hierarchies have flattened and more work is performed across functions and in cross-functional teams, peer input has gained in importance. Using 360-degree feedback data offers a much more complete view of the employee's performance and potential. While most of the feedback provided by the 360-degree tool is based on the competencies, it may also contain other information useful for assessment. For example, the retailer Best Buy has incorporated a set of items that reflects how effectively the manager has "engaged" employees—specifically, if the manager has created an environment in which employees are clear on their role expectations; have the opportunity to do what they do best; whether or not they've received recognition in the last seven days; whether or not they receive feedback, formally, on performance and development.

How these tools are applied is discussed in the following section because they play an important role in the identification process and produce simple, straightforward results. The final assessment of the individual executive or manager is reflected in an overall judgment or status decision. For example, in the case of Dell Computer, a concept called "Scaling Calls" is used to identify an individual's ability to grow into a higher-level job or to "scale" with the growth of the current job. Individuals are ranked according to a five-point scale:

1. Promote

2. Develop in place

3. Contribute in place (willing to invest more time)

4. Manage out of position

5. Are too new to call

## Lilly's "Talent ID Tool"

Almost as soon as an individual joins Lilly, the organization begins to assess talent and potential for leadership. Prior to the introduction of this tool, assessments were often highly variable across business units and functions. This instrument was created to give supervisors a common taxonomy and set of criteria from which to make their assessments. Lilly uses this assessment tool to drive more quantifiable judgments about talent that inevitably lead to the creation of a robust and diverse candidate list, or talent pools for open positions.

The six-page Talent ID Tool is used to assess more than 18,000 associates all over the world and was developed internally, with the help of outside consultants, The Lominger Group, and research from the Center for Creative Leadership. The questionnaire targets three key criteria:

1. *Performance*—relative to the seven leadership behaviors (listed previously), which track the employee's record of results over time. The evaluators look for strong development and the demonstration of management competencies.

2. *Learning agility*—tracks the individual's willingness and ability to learn new skills under first-time, tough, or different conditions.

3. *Derailment factors*—the identification of factors that might stand in the way of advancement (e.g., the employee does not value working at higher levels or does not adhere to the corporation's core values).

The form is completed by the individual's supervisor, together with a supervisor once removed, as well as previous supervisors and the peers of the individual's immediate boss. This assessment is never to be completed in isolation. It takes roughly fifteen minutes to complete, is Web based, and is available in multiple languages. The conclusions from the tool are used to determine an individual's upward potential and type of potential with the results being entered into the intranet site and formed into metrics for CEO reviews.

## Sonoco's Performance/Promotability Matrix

Sonoco believes that collecting appropriate data is the first step in identifying and managing opportunities for its talent. The divisions are asked to include the following items (nonexhaustive) in their presentations to the executive committee:

❑ Demographic breakdown of the salaried exempt workforce for that division

❑ Organization chart showing the division general manager (or corporate staff head) and his or her direct reports

❑ Succession plan chart with multiple candidates for the positions, including the division general manager

❑ "Performance/Promotability Matrix" that ranks all of the individuals on the organization chart and all the candidates from the succession chart

The "Performance/Promotability Matrix" is a nine-box matrix (Figure 3-5) that contains three levels of performance and three levels of promotability. Each division reviews its succession planning candidates and plots them into one of the nine boxes on the matrix.

The data for these succession assessments tend to be from several sources. One source is the supervisor's personal assessment of the individual using her observations, along with performance data. The performance data itself is often quite broad—in other words, not simply assessments of financial or schedule targets. It frequently includes information on staff turnover and customer satisfaction scores and so forth. An effective talent review for succession planning always involves "multiple points of view." In

**Promotability**

| | | 1 | 2 | 3 |
|---|---|---|---|---|
| **Performance** | **1** | Highly promotable within organization; significant leadership potential<br><br>Exceptional performer—exceeds requirements | Promotable—one level maximum<br><br>Exceptional performer—exceeds requirements | At level<br><br>Exceptional performer—exceeds requirements |
| | **2** | Highly promotable within organization; significant leadership potential<br><br>Effective performer—fully meets requirements | Promotable—one level maximum<br><br>Effective performer—fully meets requirements | At level<br><br>Effective performer—fully meets requirements |
| | **3** | Has potential to be highly promotable within organization<br><br>Partially meets requirements<br><br>Needs improvement (new in current position) | Has potential to be promoted—one level maximum<br><br>Partially meets requirements<br><br>Needs improvement | At level<br><br>Partially meets requirements<br><br>Needs significant improvement |

Figure 3-5. Sonoco's performance/promotability matrix.

some of the best practice organizations, the manager or sponsor of a nominated high potential identifies several individuals who are at least one level above the candidate and who know the individual well. A sixty- to ninety-minute group dialogue is conducted to assess the career potential of that candidate. These reviews eventually reach up to the executive level, so that the senior individuals have a good sense of the talent below them. In this way, the "downward" assessment (supervisor to subordinate) is not entirely dependent on the one senior viewpoint.

## Bank of America

At Bank of America, succession planning is part of a larger associate and talent planning system at play and is also one of four core corporate planning process, the others being strategy, risk, and financial.

The associate and talent planning processes are as follows (see Figure 3-6):

❑ *Between January and February* is when setting individual annual goals and objectives is finalized and quarterly performance review cycles for the current year is established. It is also during this first quarter of a calendar year when the performance discussion between the associates and their manager is completed. Sources of data used for establishing performance ratings include the individuals' performance results versus written goals for the previous year (the "what"), 360-degree feedback results against the leadership model to help determine performance ratings on the "how," and verbal feedback and input from key business partners and stakeholders.

❑ *Between July and August*, the "formal" succession planning reviews between the CEO and his top twenty-four business

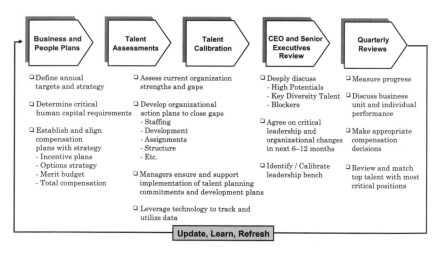

Figure 3-6. Building a strong leadership bench through continuous succession planning at Bank of America.

leaders take place. These are two-hour sessions each, during which the CEO reviews each organization's current performance, requirements for future performance, leadership talent bench gaps with plans for closing these. The group then makes decisions on critical talent moves to take place over the next twelve to eighteen months. In these CEO reviews, Bank of America uses a simple process built around a two- to three-page document (called internally an "organizational overview") that each executive produces and around which the two-hour conversation is focused.

The objective of such a minimal amount of paperwork is to drive focused discussion and to facilitate decisions, rather than having a bureaucratic process netting minimal actionable results. The document includes an organizational chart with the names of associates, their performance and potential ratings, their current total compensation, location, job title, and the line executive they support, in the case of support functions. In addition, all direct reports (DRs) to the line-of-business (LOB) executives are stack ranked and discussed thoroughly in the meetings both on current and future potential. Also, on the first page are key metrics like diversity and demographics, which are especially important to the bank's achieving its strategy of having a leadership bench that is ahead of the customer demographics. Page two compares individuals in like jobs, using an internally generated "job complexity profile" that helps ensure that the right talent is in the right role and is being compensated accordingly. This page also lists 360-degree feedback results and comparative data as well as possible moves that will be made over the next twelve to twenty-four months.

❑ The output of these two-hour conversations is documented by Executive/Leadership Development staff who then help the LOB leaders execute on these commitments.

# Focusing Efforts: Determining the "Mission-Critical" Positions

One of the vital roles of succession management is to help the organization understand what its critical management positions are. In other words, for what essential jobs do we need to be developing talent? Every firm needs to know if it is on top of the current supply of talent for these positions and what is needed for their development. As noted in Chapter 1, in the old days of succession management, it was believed that only the executive roles were truly critical.

Organizations today are more conscious of the fact that additional roles down the hierarchy may also be "mission critical." Therefore, the best succession management processes specifically target these "mission-critical" or linchpin roles. These are positions that are absolutely essential to the firm's success, typically difficult to fill, and are rarely stand-alone. For example, in a retail organization, they might range from regional managers all the way down to store managers of flagship locations. In a professional services firm, partners and senior managers would be typical linchpin roles. As William Rothwell points out, linchpin positions deserve special attention because they "represent strategically vital leverage points . . . which when they are left vacant . . . the organization will not be able to meet or exceed customer expectations, confront competition successfully, or follow through on efforts of crucial long-term significance."[6]

Rothwell offers several useful means for identifying these positions.[7] The first is to ask, "How significant are the consequences of having this particular position vacant?" If the consequences have a pronounced negative impact (such as critical decisions not being made or customer needs going unmet or operations functioning poorly), then it is likely to be a "mission critical" role.

A second approach is to examine each function on the organizational chart, asking two questions: (1) How does this function contribute uniquely to the organization's mission? and (2) If the leader in this function were gone, could it still operate effectively? Answers to the first question shed light on the magnitude of the role's contribution to firm performance. Answers to the second shed further light on whether the knowledge possessed by the leader in that particular position is unique—in other words, very difficult to replace or substitute for. It may also suggest that the scale and complexity of the role is such that other staff members collectively cannot make up for the key person's absence.

A third means to identify linchpin positions is to canvas the executive team asking them individually the following question: "What positions under your responsibility are so critical, that if they suddenly became vacant, your organization would face major problems in achieving results?"

A fourth means is to look at history and identify times when the departure of the incumbent in a particular role resulted in serious organizational problems. Were they in difficult-to-fill positions, or did they possess hard-to-find, unique knowledge and skills?

The final approach is to perform "network charting." This process involves taking a recent decision of critical importance to the firm and tracing it back to all the major contributors to that decision. Whom did the ultimate decision maker turn to for information—what positions and which individuals? The assumption is that tracing back to the various sources leads to insights about linchpin roles and individuals.

To illustrate the criteria using one of our best practice companies, Dow collectively reviewed all 250 executive positions and evaluated each using the following criteria to determine its "corporate critical" roles:

❑ The role is not subject to elimination or restructuring in the event of the incumbent's departure.

❑ Smooth, rapid transition and management continuity is critical.

❑ The role is critical to the success of the company.

## Determining the Talent Pools

With an understanding of the positions that are "mission critical," the next challenge is to categorize high-potential talent for them by using the identification and assessment tools. While the ultimate goal of succession management is to find one-to-one alignments between individual employees and vacant positions, best practice corporations are finding the formation of talent pools to be an effective real-world approach. This is especially true for positions below the executive level. (At the executive level, it is still appropriate to have a smaller slate of designated individuals.) Talent pools increase the visibility of talent among the business units and provide a starting place for making decisions about talent movement. The size and scope of talent pools differ among organizations and can be categorized by department, job, geography, and level in the hierarchy. In talent pools, high-potential employees are grouped by criteria such as skill set or promotion readiness.

For example, one of Dell's two pools is focused on talent at the corporate level, while the other exists to classify talent at the business unit or functional level. PanCanadian had A and B talent categories that identified employees with high potential in business versus high potential within professional and technical positions. Sonoco's eight pools are divided by division or business unit. As is always the case in this book, our goal is not to prescribe a specific approach for all organizations, but to expose the reader to multiple best practices that may be imported in a manner appropriate to each company's unique situation.

To determine who gets into a particular talent pool, a formal review is conducted by all of the best practices companies. Generally, the senior managers review their direct reports and complete a talent assessment of all of these individuals. Their conclusions and recommendations are synthesized and presented to a senior review group to illustrate their function's or operating group's bench strengths and needs. This presentation includes a review of the high potentials, how many are well placed, how many are ready for developmental assignments in the near term, and where the staffing gaps and vulnerabilities are. It also describes action plans for individuals based on their strengths, vulnerabilities, and job assignment opportunities. All of the results of the function or business unit are rolled up to either the senior most executive of the function or to the president of the business unit, so that they obtain a snapshot of the talent bench in their entire organization.

At Bank of America, talent pools are basically focused on future general managers who have versatility to lead various different lines of business or critical support functions. These individuals are identified by the CEO and the head of Human Resources after all twenty-four annual talent reviews are completed. They are put into a pool called "corporate resources" and are provided with unique experiences, new job assignments, very targeted and thorough assessment, and development planning (run internally by Executive Development) to "test" and "measure" their ability to successfully take on more senior or broader enterprise responsibilities in the near future. Are they really leadership bench?

The pool of "corporate resources" usually consists of no more than thirty-five to fifty senior leaders annually. The results of the assessments and their growth against their identified development needs are reviewed and tracked by Ken Lewis, and when senior roles become vacant, it is these top leaders to whom he first looks to fill many of the top positions.

# Sample Best Practice Approaches to Talent Pools

As mentioned above, Dell Computers breaks its two talent pools into corporate level pools (global corporate talent) and business unit level pools (functional high potentials). Employees designated as global corporate talent are profiled and reviewed by the Office of the Chairman and are individuals with the capability to run significant portions of a function or business and to leverage skills or experience on a global basis. This pool is always kept to fewer than 100 individuals. Dell invests a significant amount of resources and senior management time in the global corporate talent pool. Further, the company tracks the movement and development of the global corporate talent pool on a quarterly basis and reports the results to the Office of the Chairman. Dell business units also have functional high-potential programs that identify talent deeper within their organizational structures, but these are generally reviewed on the business unit level, not by the OCC.

Lilly has three talent pools. The first two are the general manager and product team leader pools and are composed of individuals who have strong cross-functional leadership talent. These roles require people who can lead across multiple disciplines in multiple cultural settings. While these individuals have typically come from sales and marketing roles, each function at Lilly contributes talent to these pools.

A third pool is for individuals who need an international assignment added to their experience base. Lilly believes that one of its strongest developmental roles is an international assignment, where an individual is placed in a new business context and is forced to understand new ways of achieving results. This type of assignment is often viewed by individuals as a career highlight.

Due to the high cost of these types of developmental assignments, they are reserved for the highest talent. Individuals nominated for these pools must have at least executive potential and must be supported by their career home function.

Sonoco uses eight talent pools that are divided by function, grouping its talent into the following categories:

1. Country managers (foreign countries)

2. Vice president, director level, for sales and marketing

3. Manager level, for sales and marketing

4. Vice president, director level, for manufacturing

5. Finance/IT positions

6. Human resources

7. Technology and engineering

8. Purchasing and other staff pools

When a position becomes available at Sonoco, corporate HR conducts a search across the organization for those individuals who have been identified as potential successors for that position. A cross-corporation pool is then created and the potential successor is extracted from it. Corporate HR also examines the number of individuals in each pool who are in the high-potential block on the Performance/Promotability Matrix and creates a corporate-wide listing. This provides HR and the executive committee with a high-level view of the whole organization. Sonoco estimates that it has the right person ready to step into its job openings 80 to 90 percent of the time.

# Insights from the Research

1. Best practice organizations begin the identification process by establishing competencies for each position. These are established core competencies (company-wide) and core leadership competencies (for succession management). A single model is typically used for the top levels of the organization. Competency models are most effective when they focus on a few items that set effective leaders in the organization apart from less effective ones, rather than listing every positive trait that all leaders might possess. Otherwise, the rigor of developing competencies is often compromised by adding in too many variables that hinder effective utilization.

2. Competencies work best when the behaviors that accompany them are identified in concrete terms that make the assessment process less open to wide subjective interpretations by observers/raters. Managers who have been provided training to understand and identify a firm's competencies are likely to be more effective in the assessment process.

3. A key aspect of identifying high-potential talent is the gathering of adequate information about employees through identification tools such as 360-degree feedback. This "multi-rater" assessment provides richer information and less opportunity for bias or inaccuracy than reliance on the views of the boss working alone. In some firms the 360-degree feedback is becoming a vital part of the performance management and developmental planning processes.

4. Grouping high-potential employees into talent pools has proven to be an effective method for assuring that the right person is available when a position opens up. The logic behind this is simply a recognition that more detailed attention can be focused on a subset of managers rather than attempting to include everyone with a basic standard. Moreover, there is evidence that greater returns are achieved by providing special opportunities for individuals who have the capability for greatest growth from the special developmental opportunities provided for them. Mechanisms for insuring fairness, multiple perspectives, and regular review are vital if a talent pool is to win the support of managers who are being reviewed and those who are monitoring the pool.

# Notes

1 D. C. McClelland, "Testing for Competence Rather Than for Intelligence," *American Psychologist* (Jan. 1973), pp. 1–14.

2 R. Boyatzis, *The Competent Manager* (New York: Wiley, 1982).

3 Jessica Sweeney-Platt, Corporate Leadership Council Research Studies, Washington, D.C., December 2001.

4   Donna Rodriguez, Rita Patel, Andrea Bright, Donna Gregory, and Marilyn K. Gowing, "Developing Competency Models to Promote Integrated Human Resource Practices," *Human Resource Management* 41/3, (Sept. 1, 2002), p. 309.

5   Gary Hamel and C. K. Prahalad, "The Core Competence of the Corporation," *Harvard Business Review*, May–June 1990, pp. 79–91.

6   William J. Rothwell, *Effective Succession Planning* (New York: AMACOM, 2001), p. 172.

7   Ibid., pp. 173–75.

# Chapter Four

# LINKING SUCCESSION TO DEVELOPMENT

Toward the end of the last economic boom, the management consulting firm of McKinsey & Company published a study that it called "The War for Talent."[1] During the tumultuous last days of the 1990s and into the early days of the new century, finding qualified management talent loomed as one of the major challenges of thoughtful executives. To probe the details of this challenge, McKinsey sent thousands of questionnaires to managers in various industries throughout the nation. Eighteen companies were visited by study leaders, who interviewed middle and upper managers. The study's most important finding was that the senior leaders of the best companies were virtually obsessed with the

75

talent issue, constantly recruiting top performers from other companies and compensating them handsomely. We believe that the
emphasis on talent is still a source of competitive advantage, but
we can learn from the excesses of some firms. Once on board,
McKinsey recommended that these stars be placed on a fast track.
"Bet on the natural athletes, the ones with the strongest intrinsic
skills," a General Electric executive is quoted as saying.

So far, so good. But as with anything else, this principle can
be pushed too far. As with any management belief, there is a
right way and a wrong way to go about succession management.
Malcolm Gladwell, in a 2002 article published in *The New Yorker*
called "The Talent Myth," provides a case study of the wrong
way:

> In the modern corporation, the system is considered
> only as strong as its stars, and, in the past few years,
> this message has been preached by consultants and
> management gurus all over the world. None, however,
> have spread the word quite so ardently as McKinsey,
> and, of all its clients, one firm took the talent mind-set
> closest to heart. It was a company where McKinsey con-
> ducted twenty separate projects, where McKinsey's bill-
> ings topped ten million dollars a year, where a
> McKinsey director regularly attended board meetings,
> and where the C.E.O. himself was a former McKinsey
> partner. The company, of course, was Enron.[2]

One of McKinsey's core recommendations is for employers to
sort employees into three groups. Those in the top group are put
on the fast track to leadership in both assignments and compensation. Those in the middle group are encouraged toward future
growth. Those in the last group are pressured to "shape up or ship

out." This process is officially called "differentiation and affirmation," but was referred to at Enron as "rank and yank":

> Enron followed this advice almost to the letter, setting up internal Performance Review Committees. The members got together twice a year and graded each person in their section on ten separate criteria, using a scale of one to five. . . . Those graded at the top of their unit received bonuses two-thirds higher than those in the next thirty percent; those who ranked at the bottom received no bonuses and no extra stock options—and in some cases were pushed out.[3]

Such hard-nosed tactics were apparently reflective of the overall corporate culture at Enron, and they are no doubt practiced elsewhere. While Enron is an extreme example, the very public downfall of that company would suggest that its approach to succession management was not effective in establishing long-term stability and productivity within the corporation. If that's true, the next question we must ask is, "Why?"

The answer may be found in another study conducted by the Corporate Leadership Council in 2001. Based on responses from 8,000 corporate leaders from thirty-one firms across six industries in eight countries, the "Voice of the Leader" study attempted to serve as "A Quantitative Analysis of Leadership Bench Strength and Development Strategies."[4] For our purposes, its key findings are most intriguing when presented in reverse order:

> 6. Companies with above-average leadership bench strength enjoy above-average thirty-six-month revenue growth relative to industry peer group.

| |
|---|
| 5. Organizations that successfully reallocate their development resources to meet leaders' needs can measurably improve the strength of their leadership bench. |
| 4. Many organizations struggle to implement the most important leadership development programs effectively and would benefit by reallocating their development resources to meet leaders' needs. |
| 3. Feedback and relationship (coaching, mentoring) programs are the most effective leadership development strategy. |
| 2. Many leadership teams are weakest in the skill area that matters most, leading companies to look for solutions to the leadership development challenge. |
| 1. More than 8,000 leaders report that people-management skills are the most important attributes of effective leadership, outranking strategic management, personal characteristics, or day-to-day business management. |

Source:  Corporate Leadership Council, "Voice of the Leader: A Quantitative Analysis of Leadership Bench Strength and Development Strategies." Washington, D.C.: Corporate Executive Board, 2001, pp. vi–xi.

In other words, the study found that corporations benefit quantitatively when they allocate their resources to partner with their employees to help them gain the skills they need to become effective managers. This partnership approach lies in stark contrast to the "rank and yank" approach—or Enron model—in which the burden is placed on the employee to "shape up or ship out."

Ironically, the "rank and yank" approach is antithetical to the underlying premise of the "war for talent" concept, which states that talented employees are a corporation's most valuable commodity and are therefore worth compensating at a high level in order to attract and retain. This scenario suggests, rightly, that there is a limited pool of really talented people out there and that finding and keeping good people is difficult to do. The merciless, survival-of-the-fittest attitude of the "rank and yank" approach suggests just the opposite: that employees are expendable if they don't meet the highest standards, as if there were a line of better qualified candidates just waiting to get in the door. Even in troubled economic times, finding the right person for a key job can be a difficult challenge.

Most importantly, the survival-of-the-fittest approach is, by its very nature, short-sighted. It ignores the fundamental question of the "war for talent" concept: Where are tomorrow's leaders coming from? The answer is the same as it has always been: They are more likely to be coming from inside your company. They are all around you. They have innate talents and abilities that you may not yet be able to see. They will mature at different times, in different ways, and at their own pace. They will emerge as leaders in sometimes subtle ways and perhaps only within a limited, yet crucial, sphere.

If the organization and its managers are not helping them grow, they may remain stunted. If no one recognizes their potential, it may go to waste. If no one notices when they flourish, they may leave for more fertile ground. The model shown in Figure 4-1 captures how one company thinks about this cycle. For Bank of America, what distinguishes the best-in-class in talent management is the organization's capability to select the right individuals for the most critical roles based on business needs and strategy; then to provide an integrated set of interventions (programs, processes, and initiatives) that supports the new leader's transition into the role, and additionally promotes the new leader's growth and development and encourages high levels of performance.

Figures 4-2 and 4-3 are from the Corporate Leadership Council's "Voice of the Leader" study.[5]

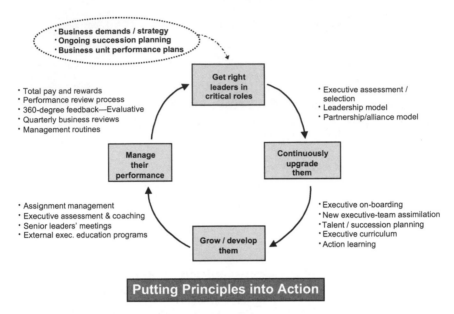

Figure 4-1. Building a strong leadership bench: Integrated processes drive the development agenda at Bank of America.

According to the respondents in the Council's study, providing the opportunity and authority to accomplish challenging objects as well the creation of specific personal developmental plans were the most effective ways of developing leaders. Standardized skill courses were seen as being the least important. This data portrays a clear and significant preference for learning by doing rather than learning just in case that knowledge might be required.

# Weaving Development into Succession

The APQC study of best practice organizations found unanimous agreement that simply identifying high-potential employees is not enough. Each of these companies devotes a great deal of attention

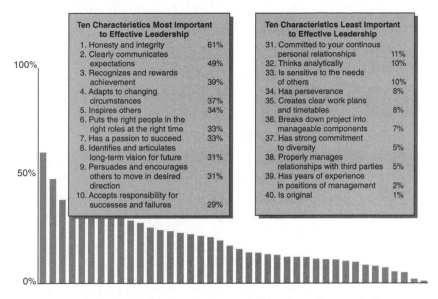

| Ten Characteristics Most Important to Effective Leadership | | Ten Characteristics Least Important to Effective Leadership | |
|---|---|---|---|
| 1. Honesty and integrity | 61% | 31. Committed to your continous personal relationships | 11% |
| 2. Clearly communicates expectations | 49% | 32. Thinks analytically | 10% |
| 3. Recognizes and rewards achievement | 39% | 33. Is sensitive to the needs of others | 10% |
| 4. Adapts to changing circumstances | 37% | 34. Has perseverance | 8% |
| 5. Inspires others | 34% | 35. Creates clear work plans and timetables | 8% |
| 6. Puts the right people in the right roles at the right time | 33% | 36. Breaks down project into manageable components | 7% |
| 7. Has a passion to succeed | 33% | 37. Has strong commitment to diversity | 5% |
| 8. Identifies and articulates long-term vision for future | 31% | 38. Properly manages relationships with third parties | 5% |
| 9. Persuades and encourages others to move in desired direction | 31% | 39. Has years of experience in positions of management | 2% |
| 10. Accepts responsibility for successes and failures | 29% | 40. Is original | 1% |

Figure 4-2. The most and least important skills and attributes of effective leadership. Source: Corporate Leadership Council, "Voice of the Leader: A Quantitative Analysis of Leadership Bench Strength and Development Strategies." Washington, D.C.: Corporate Executive Board, 2001, p. 10B.

to developmental activities for their high-potential employees, and they dedicate ample resources to the process. Furthermore, all of the best practice companies in this study utilize specific and individualized development plans for each employee identified as a future leader.

As seen from the identification process outlined in Chapter 3, business unit or functional leaders are responsible (with the help of a human resources partner) for the deliverables of their group's succession plan. At Bank of America, it is clearly understood that it is every executives' responsibility to grow and develop future leaders for the company. While the business unit executives are held accountable, they are assisted with the process by tools and support from the human resources and leadership development partners aligned to their business unit. The same

| Development Program | Overall Rank |
|---|---|
| Amount of decision-making authority | 1 |
| Creating leadership development plan | 2 |
| Interacting with peers | 3 |
| Meeting with an executive coach | 4 |
| Meeting with a mentor | 5 |
| Feedback | 6 |
| Turning around a struggling business | 7 |
| People-management skills courses | 8 |
| Working in new functional areas | 9 |
| Working in foreign countries | 10 |
| Working in new lines of business | 11 |
| Launching a new business | 12 |
| Number of direct reports | 13 |
| Quality of direct reports | 14 |
| Off-site seminars in business skills | 15 |
| Technical skills courses | 16 |
| Business skills courses | 17 |

Figure 4-3. Rank order of development by importance score.
Source: Corporate Leadership Council, "Voice of the Leader: A Quantitative
Analysis of Leadership Bench Strength and Development Strategies."
Washington, D.C.: Corporate Executive Board, 2001, p. 34B.

holds true on the back end of the process. Once business unit
leaders have identified high-potential talent, they are responsible
(with the help of a human resources partner) for making sure
development plans and activities are carried out.

Interestingly, developmental activities do not dramatically
differ from one best practice organization to the next. In every
case, these companies:

❑ Invest the majority of their time and resources on top-tier
talent (executive-level talent)

❑ Participate in some form of mentoring and/or coaching
and/or survey feedback, whether formal or informal

❑ Engage in action learning, including special job assignments

❑ Attempt to place high-potentials across the organization

In addition, virtually all of these companies use the same readiness indicator as a decision-making guide for assigning development. (The three main indicators are ready-now candidates, ready-in-one-year candidates, and ready-in-the-future [two to five years] candidates). Bank of America uses ready now and ready in one to two years as indicators of bench strength readiness. However, over the last several years, more emphasis has been placed on the ready-now category (within twelve months able to move to a new assignment) for reasons related to the increased pace of change, growing complexity, and demands being placed on leaders, as well as the company's growth rates. This nearer-term emphasis has been found to be a more effective approach for several reasons.

Focusing more heavily on the ready-now bench strength has provided a more realistic view of the current and future leadership pipeline since speculation about longer-term potential is removed. Secondly, it has forced greater clarity on the "real" expectations of leaders versus staying at the hypothetical "what will it take three to five years out to succeed." Thirdly, it has driven greater accountability into the overall talent management process. Senior managers surfacing up names as "ready now replacements" know that (a) their people are fair game to be moved to a new role and (b) they are immediately accountable for their recommendations.

Figure 4-4 shows the breakdown of development activities employed internally by the best practice organizations compared

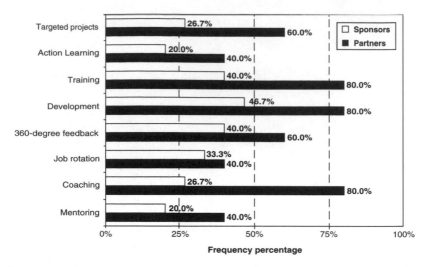

Figure 4-4. Succession management process design with regard to internal developmental activities.

to the control group in the APQC study. The graph demonstrates that the use of fundamental developmental activities (most notably, coaching, targeted projects, and training and development) is far more prevalent in best practice corporations than in the control group.

# The Tools They Use

The APQC study found four major common factors in how best practice organizations engage their current and future leaders in developmental activities:

1. They believe that the most important developmental activity is job assignments/work experience. As a result, they spend considerable time in balancing the corporation's need to fill vacant or new positions with the kind of assign-

ments that will help key people grow and develop their potential. They think careful about the assignment's capacity to stretch and even "over stretch" the candidate.

For example, Bank of America weighs many factors when moving a leader to a new role for their development. In addition to what the individual needs to develop for his own growth, it considers factors such as job size, scale, scope (number of FTEs, Revenue, Revenue per FTE, growth measures, etc.) as well as department or market conditions, customer demographics, and overall business needs (e.g., degree of organizational change needed; start-up versus productivity improvement opportunity). All of this information is put into what the bank refers to as "job complexity profiles" which in turn are used to make appropriate organizational structure and "people move" decisions—decisions that stretch leaders appropriately but also ensure they will succeed in their new roles (see Figure 4-5). Additionally the bank has several high potential programs involving "deep" assessment, coaching, and development of executives. The development recommendations from these programs ensure that leaders are assigned to the right developmental experiences, and given appropriate coaches and mentors and the right special project opportunities for stretch and development with current and future needs in mind.

2. They use a variety of developmental activities, such as mentoring, coaching, job rotation, traditional educational programs, and formalized feedback processes.

3. They are trying new approaches to development, including special assignments, action learning, and Web-based educational activities.

Figure 4-5. Assignment management: Developing top talent through *stretch* assignments at Bank of America.

4. They are finding that computer-based technology has expanded their ability to effectively monitor developmental activities.

## PanCanadian's Leadership Development Framework

At PanCanadian, developmental activities tie to individual development plans and are mandatory for input to the performance management process. Key talent updates and developmental opportunities are reported monthly to allow for movement and special assignment of employees. To help PanCanadian manage its developmental activities, the company created the leadership and management development framework seen in Figure 4-6.

Figure 4-6. PanCanadian's leadership and management development framework.

The framework is based on a hub-and-spoke framework in which leadership competency development is the hub. The six spokes are:

1. *Succession management,* which handles the identification of future leaders, while the other five spokes deal in one way or another with the development of those leaders. *It manages current leaders and identifies future leaders and development plans for current and future leaders.*

2. *Training,* which houses PanCanadian's Management Institute, handles in-house training, and leads new supervisor training.

3. *Performance management,* which is in charge of 360-degree feedback, accountability agreements, and performance coaching.

4. *Significant other people*, which houses mentoring (formal and informal), coaching, and the HR
   business partners.

5. *On-the-job experience*, which manages projects,
   assignments, job rotation, and networks.

6. *Stretch development opportunities*, which is in
   charge of the leadership institute and executive
   development.

Notice that only one of the six spokes is focused on
the identification of potential leaders, while each of
the other five spokes address some aspect of training and development.

Throughout the remainder of this chapter, we look at some
developmental tools in more detail. As with the identification
process, each company has developed its own unique approach to
implementing these activities. Our purpose here is not to promote
a specific approach, but to give you a sampling of best-practice
activities and programs that may spark ideas for your own organization.

## Tool #1—Internal Leadership and Executive Education

As noted above, the best practice organizations in the APQC
study all have formal internal programs in place that focus on the
further development of their top-tier executives. Dow Chemical,
for example, offers a wide variety of the executive development
opportunities (mentoring and coaching, action learning). A recent, internal study shows that participants in Dow's program im-

proved their strategic thinking, external focus, consumer orientation, and global view. An increase in compensation and performance was also reported.

At Bank of America, while the foundation of its executive development efforts remains focused on its highest performers and potentials, there are specific executive development programs and processes offered to other groups that balance the needs of the individual executive to perform to today's standards with the needs of the enterprise to perform and win in the future.

Dell and Lilly also exemplify the best practice approach to executive education. Dell focuses most of its development activities on the global corporate talent pool that houses its top talent. After talent is identified through the office of the chairman (OOC) review, business unit leaders are responsible for carrying out whatever developmental actions are designated. Through cross-organizational movement of high-potential individuals, Dell's OOC is actively involved in the career and skill development of the global corporate talent pool. Built around its competency model, Dell's executive education program blends e-learning (DellDirect) and leader-led curricula. Some noteworthy courses include Executive Level Communication, Strategic Leadership, and Strategic Management Business Simulation.

One of Lilly's most effective executive development programs is the group development review, which is mandatory for every candidate with executive director potential. Approximately 500 individuals with the highest potential are the subject of a ninety-minute conversation among supervisors. To affirm the potential of candidates and to specify development needs, feedback is taken from multiple levels of both current and previous supervision. The group discusses the strengths and weaknesses of the candidate, and then the individual's supervisor shares a summary of the results with the employee. The two of them, along with HR, are then charged with putting in place or revising the development and career plan for the candidate. The talent identification tool (discussed in Chapter 3), coupled with the group development review, validates and confirms candidate potential while providing input to both the development plan and career plan.

## Tool #2—Action Learning and Special Job Assignments

Most of the best-practice companies agree that the vast majority of learning takes place on the job. Consequently these companies have a special assignments or action learning program in place. One of the most common—and seemingly effective—approaches is a task force assignment based on real and significant issues confronting the organization.

Lilly's action learning program, the most robust among those covered by the APQC study, is called "Leadership V." Run every other year, it brings together eighteen executive potential leaders from all functions. The structured program covers a six-week time frame, during which the participants focus on a business issue chosen by the CEO. Activities include offsite meetings, presentations by subject matter experts, and team-based interviews with best practice organizations, customers, and thought leaders. The results of the interviews are then compiled, and the team generates a presentation of findings for the CEO, complete with a recommended course of action.

Dow Chemical engages its future leaders by giving special assignments and/or action learning exercises on a task force basis. Like Lilly, Dow's action learning exercises provide participants with the opportunity to study a particular topic area and present their findings to senior management. Assignments are chosen that present a challenge that can improve business results, processes, or relationships. Dow notes that these developmental exercises emphasize competency development rather than development for a specific job. Most functional or corporate projects are staffed predominately from this population. Projects around sustainable development, the corporate people (human resources) strategy, and Six Sigma are typical development opportunities.

At Bank of America, there are specific activities to which high potentials are assigned. Action learning initiatives, where they are asked to study a specific enterprise topic and present findings to senior leaders, are typical approaches. Green and black belt projects from the bank's Six-Sigma programs are also used as a means to assign top performers to highly quantifiable and large-impact projects. Task-force assignments are deployed as additional means to challenge and test top performers and highest potentials. The output of this work is closely observed by senior executives.

## Tool #3—Mentoring and Coaching

The best practice organizations in this study all participate in mentoring and coaching programs, but primarily on an informal basis. Formal coaching is usually reserved for the companies' top executive high potentials and is commonly outsourced. Dow, for example, uses an external service for its top positions. New hires at Dow are assigned a mentor, at which point the process moves forward informally. To expedite organizational fit, experienced hires are assigned a mentor as well.

Based on an internal study of their experienced executives, which found that successful mentoring was a critical factor for success in their careers, Dow is now undertaking even more systematic efforts about selecting mentors and ensuring that mentors meet regularly with their charges. In selecting a mentor, the company looks at matching interests with functional and business backgrounds, along with the mentor's desire to engage in active mentoring.

The goals of Lilly's mentoring program are to:

❑ Facilitate short- and long-term business performance by developing the executive talent pool, with particular emphasis on minorities, females, and other forms of diversity

❑ Strengthen the relational and learning skills of mentors and mentees

❑ Develop effective role models for mentoring among senior executives

❑ Further develop the competencies of mentees leading to an understanding of organizational culture, personal development, job satisfaction, and new career opportunities

❑ Create expectations for mentoring throughout the organization

❑ Identify general principles from which a culture supportive of mentoring can be built

Since its introduction in 1998, the program has had success with its targeted audience. Given the limited numbers of people who can be involved as mentors, the formalized program has been run more sporadically. Informal mentoring occurs frequently and is seen as an important part of development.

At Bank of America, coaching support is tied to individual needs of senior executives. Certain of the executive development programs offered to the bank's highest potentials at different levels in the organization include internal coaching and external coaching resources. Additionally, as leaders make their way closer to the top, their specific issues and needs become more complex and individualized, so the bank offers these senior executives top business coaches who possess both industry and business world experience.

## Tool #4—External University Courses

The best practice organizations in this study use a mix of internal and external university-based education and development courses. PanCanadian offered internal university M.B.A. courses, while Dow focuses on external, university-based educational opportunities and consortium projects.

Dow has identified numerous universities across the country that specialize in areas such as entrepreneurialism, technology, and international affairs. Dow Learning Centers worldwide have classroom activities and some select university programs at graduate business-school levels. The university-based programs are typically one- to four-week programs at institutions such as the University of Michigan, Indiana University, IMD, INSEAD, and the Thunderbird Institute (Tucson, Ariz.). Dow also takes advantage of consortium programs, in which several companies jointly cooperate in an academic program.

PanCanadian offered an internal M.B.A. program called the Management Forum. The purpose of this two-year program was to provide management education by bringing best practices to participants. The Management Forum was specifically created to align management competencies with strategic direction to meet current and future needs. PanCanadian used the forum to share existing knowledge and new findings. The forum was focused on developing three core competencies: (1) managing performance, (2) change and innovation, and (3) knowledge management.

## Tool #5—Web-Based Courses

With the vast and accessible training opportunities available through the Worldwide Web, best practice organizations are making a wide array of training courses available to their employees online. Dow and Dell, for example, both have extensive courseware available.

Dow utilizes Web-based functions to support leaders and developmental activities, as well as an online application called Learn@dow.now. Learn@dow.now is an externally developed learning and training program through which more than 600 courses are offered online. Dow reports that 14,000 courses were completed in a single week by employees. Examples of training courses available on the site include safety training, a course required for executives on respect and responsibility training, and compensation planning tools. Dow currently has sixty tools and classes available online in its internal development program. Some examples include:

❑ Ethics and compliance

❑ Foreign corrupt practices act

❑ Root Learning Maps that explain its strategy, measures, economic profit, people strategy, etc.

❑ Six Sigma

As might be expected, Dell Computer also uses online tools for executive development. DellDirect is an intranet site, available to all executives, that allows users to participate in conversation groups, online interviews, book signings, literature, courses, orientation materials, and speaker slides.

Lilly University offers employees a variety of online training, career development, and knowledge management tools to address their learning needs through an all-employee portal called "my-Learning." Employees can make connections directly to training modules, register for classroom training, identify internal experts in a variety of topics, update their internal resume and expertise profile, or search internal and external publications by topic.

## Tool #6—Career Planning and Individual Profiling

The APQC study found that more and more emphasis is being put on career planning and individual profiling as it relates to succession management. For example, individual development plans are used by all of the best practice organizations in the study, as opposed to only 60 percent of the control group. Similarly, career planning is used by 60 percent of the best practice organizations, but only 30 percent of the control group. The best practice organizations in the study look closely at employees' career preferences and try to match their interests and career development to a future job. Employee career preferences can influence the development process, and employee preferences are honored where possible.

For example, Dell adopted a career development model that assists individuals in planning their careers through four stages. The first stage is for new hires to understand how to approach

Dell's direct-selling business model. The second and third stages focus on learning how to contribute independently and collaboratively through leadership. The last stage centers on gaining organizational leadership (Figure 4-7).

At Dow Chemical, employee development plans are encouraged but not mandatory for all employees. On the other hand, written development plans are required of their high potentials or "future leaders." Upon nomination as a "future leader," the individual must submit the written development plan, which must then be reviewed by the corporate operating board. Development and implementation of the plan are the responsibility of the employee's superior, but other members of the corporate operating board may be engaged to create cross-business, cross-function, or cross-geographical opportunities. In addition, the required employee development plans for future leaders address identified competency or experience gaps.

Lilly fosters a culture that values and encourages professional development. Where HR previously owned and managed resumes and development plans, all employees and their supervisors are now responsible to create those same documents online. Embedded in the company's annual performance management process, it is essential that the content of both is linked together. The resume details positions held, positions of interest, status levels, current location, and potential relocation information, while the development plan is comprised of both short-term and long-term goals designed to help guide employees in ways of improving their performance and overall potential.

Lilly's largest development program is the "group development review." In addition to a range of background data, participants provide resumes that detail positions held, positions of interest, status levels, current location, and potential relocation

# Business Acumen

*Knows how businesses work; knowledgeable in current and possible future policies, practices, trends, and information affecting his/her business and organization; knows the competition; is aware of how strategies and tactics work in the marketplace.*

| Stage I<br>Helping and Learning | Stage II<br>Contributing Independently<br>(Personal Leadership) | Stage III<br>Contributing Through Others<br>(Local Leadership) | Stage IV<br>Leading Through Vision<br>(Organizational Leadership) |
|---|---|---|---|
| • Learns how his or her work relates to Dell's overall business strategy<br>• Demonstrates a basic understanding of business practice and actively seeks out additional information<br>• Is beginning to build relationships within the local workgroup that will develop his/her business understanding | • Acts with an understanding of how the marketplace drives the business<br>• Demonstrates an understanding of financial, economic, market, and organizational data<br>• Stays abreast of industry developments and outside factors that may influence Dell's business | • Explains the organization's business climate, customers, competitors, and competitive advantage to others<br>• Rigorously monitors quarterly targets, finances, the market, and the competition<br>• Evaluates competitors' technology strategies and their relevance for Dell<br>• Encourages others to stay up-to-date in their knowledge of what is going on in other parts of the company and industry | • Reinforces the importance of integrating financial business practices (cost control, P&L, inventory management, etc.) in key business matters<br>• Demonstrates a strong understanding of the industry's threats and opportunities<br>• Sponsors efforts within the organization to leverage emerging business opportunities<br>• Anticipates long-term global business trends and how they will affect the market |

Figure 4-7. Dell's staged model for development.

information. The supervisors discuss the strengths and weaknesses of the candidate and then share the results with the candidate. With the help of HR, the supervisor is then charged with putting in place a development and career plan for the candidate. Employee development plans form directly from this performance management process. The development plan is produced to assist the employee in improving in her current role, while at the same time creating a longer-term plan to help reach the potential for advancement.

Within Sonoco, corporate HR discusses the development plans for the appropriate individuals with its HR managers. This discussion focuses on the best way to deliver development information on an individual basis. The divisions are then responsible for following up to ensure that the development plans are carried out, with corporate HR providing oversight.

One reason for the increased use of development plans is that managers in all of these organizations now have access to online succession management tools, software, and enhanced data warehousing. In addition, this access benefits the administrators by allowing them to work from one central repository of succession management information, and by allowing them to look at data in real time. Employees also benefit by having access to more information and control of their employee profile. In the cases of Lilly and Sonoco, employees are responsible for ensuring that all the pertinent data is available and correct on their employee resume before evaluation. They have access to their performance management data and access to the results of the 360-degree feedback process. In some cases, employees are even responsible for scheduling succession management review meetings. The succession management package that is used for review is rich with information about employees, helping administrators to make better, more informed decisions. Some of the types of information collected by the best practice organizations include:

- ❑ Biographical information (including a photo of the employee)

- ❑ Career history (internal and external positions held, reporting levels, locations, etc.)

- ❑ Positions of interest

- ❑ Potential relocation information

- ❑ Performance evaluation information (including results of 360-degree feedback)

- ❑ Competency strengths and opportunities

- ❑ Development plans

At Bank of America, all associates are expected to have a written individual development plan. Each associate and her manager discuss the plan as part of her quarterly performance review discussions.

For senior executives, the development plans are more focused on improvements against specific assessment feedback received (e.g., 360-degree feedback results against the company's leadership model/competencies) as well as tied more directly toward preparing the executive for a next assignment. These executives' 360-degree feedback results, personal development preferences, as well as specific and tactical development action plans are tracked as part of the quarterly performance review discussions. For the best performers and highest potentials, these plans are shared and

discussed in detail with the CEO as part of his detailed business
and organizational succession planning reviews.

## Tool #7—Performance Management and 360-Degree Feedback

Performance management and 360-degree feedback are linked
throughout the succession management process and are the two
main tools used by the best practice organizations to place employees into development plans. These two tools are tied together
and based on core and leadership competencies. Several of the
benchmark companies tie their use of performance management
and 360-degree feedback together, but most use the results of performance management for compensation, promotion decisions,
and some development. They employ the results of 360-degree
feedback for development purposes. We sense that the use of 360-
degree feedback for assessment purposes is a relatively new development, but the benchmark firms were more likely to align these
two programs than the sponsor companies.

Lilly uses COMPASS, a 360-degree feedback tool designed to
assess its seven leadership behaviors. The 360-degree process is
primarily used for development. Employees are strongly encouraged to share the results of the 360-degree evaluation with their
supervisors and to leverage the feedback as they update their development plans. While the online tool was once available for
only the executive group, it is now required for all 3,300 management level employees.

Dell Computer's 360-degree feedback system is composed of a
survey that collects detailed, behavior-based data on an individual's job behavior from his boss(es), peers, direct reports, and customers. Throughout the system, individuals identify gaps in their

behavior and then develop steps to improve performance. The data is owned by the individual and used for developmental purposes only. The individual is responsible for sharing his key learnings with a manager and jointly developing a plan to address the goals.

At Dow, all employees are expected to engage in three performance activities:

1. Annual goals

2. Performance reviews/discussions

3. Employee development discussions resulting in plans

Two tools are offered that involve input from multiple sources:

1. *360-degree development feedback,* which is based on the competency profile of the individual. This is for developmental purposes and is owned by the employee. The employee, however, is encouraged to share the results and action plans with her supervisor.

2. *Performance excellence feedback,* which is based on the individual's goals. This is for performance feedback and is owned by the employee and the supervisor.

At Sonoco, each division prepares for its succession planning meeting in March. Employees must update and complete their performance management documents in this first quarter. Performance management documents review four dimensions for each employee: role objectives, core and leadership competencies, career and development plans, and general comments. During the year, the Sonoco employees update the performance management document, discuss it with supervisors, modify it again, and have periodic reviews. The completed documents are designed to show the path the employee is on and the key activities/issues the individual needs to address.

At Bank of America, performance management is made quite clear for its top 5,000 managers. It is about achieving the *right results the right way. Right results* (the what) are measured and defined by written, stretch financial, shareholder, associate, and customer goals and metrics; *right way* (the how) is measured by the leadership behaviors demonstrated to achieve the results. In fact, the results of the executive's 360-degree feedback around the company's leadership model are the foundation for the rating on the "how." These results inform each executive about leadership performance relative to an internal peer group as well as help to focus on development plans (refer to the company's nine-box performance grid). In the end, top leaders must minimally meet or exceed both dimensions to be recognized and rewarded appropriately. Those who do will get the lion's share of compensation and career opportunities.

# Conclusion and Summary Insights from the Research

What we see in our study is that the best practice organizations are doing precisely what the 8,000 corporate leaders of the Leadership Council study recommend: devoting adequate resources to training and development. They use a variety of methods, and they quantify performance as much as possible. As Malcolm Gladwell writes:

> The only rigorous way to assess performance, according to human-resources specialists, is to use criteria

that are as specific as possible. Managers are supposed to take detailed notes on their employees throughout the year, in order to remove subjective personal reactions from the process of assessment. You can grade someone's performance only if you know their performance. And, in the freewheeling culture of Enron, this was all but impossible. People deemed "talented" were constantly being pushed into new jobs and given new challenges. Annual turnover from promotions was close to twenty per cent.[6]

As we noted in Chapter 3, many firms, including our best practice partners, address the challenge of specificity by developing competency models of the attributes associated with successful leaders in their specific company's environment. The degree to which an individual is seen as possessing these competencies may suggest the individual's potential for continued success in the firm. When an assessment indicates that specific competencies are rated low, it indicates a developmental need for the individual. In our closing chapter, we discuss in more detail the limitations of these competency models for assessing potential and future needs. For now, we would point out that one major challenge in using competency models is that they are typically built on those attributes that have been associated with current and past successful leaders in the firm. In today's rapidly changing environment, the more optimal approach would be to look for those competencies that will be required for future success.

Best practice organizations emphasize the importance of specific, individualized development plans for each employee because a key to succession management is the *tailored* development of high-potential employees. Individual plans dictate which developmental activities are needed. Typically, there is also a mechanism in place to ensure that the employees get the developmental activities they need. This mechanism often involves a human resources partner who oversees employee participation in developmental activities. In an increasing number of firms, the employee is responsible for keeping the data in his personnel file up to date with any specific developmental activities that have been completed, such as educational courses or coaching assignments. New job assignments are more likely to be monitored and posted by the human resources team.

Best practice partners rely on the fundamental developmental activities of job assignments, special projects, action learning, coaching, training, and mentoring more frequently and utilize all developmental activities to a much greater extent than did our control organizations. While there was little that is truly innovative in the practices utilized by our benchmark firms, the comprehensive use of multiple approaches and the degree to which they are integrated into a consistent, aligned system seemed to mark the major difference between the excellent and the ordinary. Action learning and coaching programs seem to be used increasingly. These initiatives are often included as part of a customized learning initiative aimed at the high potential talent pool.

In our opinion, the best firms are able to achieve the illusive concept of synergy when a learning program is designed to support a new strategic direction and to provide developmental problem solving and implementation experience for high potentials at the same time. As one anonymous respondent commented, "Rather than bring in a major consulting firm to solve a problem, we prefer to give our best and brightest some tools to address the problem and turn them loose. Their solution is more likely to reflect an understanding of our environment, and they will be around to help with the implementation. Moreover, their new skills get embedded in our organization rather than going out the door when the project ends.

# Notes

1   Ed Michaels, Helen Handfield-Jones, Beth Axelrod, *The War for Talent* (Boston: Harvard Business School Press, 2001).

2   Malcolm Gladwell, "The Talent Myth," *The New Yorker*, July 22, 2002, p. 28.

3   Ibid., p. 29.

4   Corporate Leadership Council, "Voice of the Leader: A Quantitative Analysis of Leadership Bench Strength and Development Strategies." Washington, D.C.: Corporate Executive Board, 2001.

5   Ibid, pp. 10B and 34B, respectively.

6   Gladwell, p. 28.

# Chapter Five

# MEASURING AND ASSURING LONG-TERM SUCCESS

Developing leadership talent is a long-term investment. Unlike the "replacement" mindset of succession management of the past, today's systems must take the longer view. Their effectiveness is determined by their ability to move talented individuals at an *appropriate pace* into the *right developmental opportunities* over the *span of their careers.* With this aim in mind, tracking the progress of individual participants is a necessary dimension of a best practice succession process. At the same, the most successful systems must also measure their own record at identifying developmental opportunities, filling them with the right people at the right time, and spotting looming shortages or gaps in both talent and in developmental positions. Of course, this awareness is meaningless unless steps are taken to rectify these gaps quickly.

As we saw in the identification and development phases, best practice organizations employ a variety of methods of measurement and assessment to ensure that these outcomes are achieved. In many cases, both quantitative and qualitative methods of assessment are employed to provide the broadest and most fine-grained range of perspectives on the system's real effectiveness. As with the other dimensions of succession management, the monitoring and assessment phase of succession management takes place on an ongoing, cyclical basis.

Finally, the long-term success of these processes is the product of the owners' willingness to constantly revisit and, in turn, redesign the systems themselves. A mindset that "once in place, always in place" is a dangerous one with succession planning. The best practice organizations employed the Japanese notion of *kaizen* or continuous improvement in both processes and content.

## What Is Measured?

In terms of quantitative measurements of system effectiveness, the most frequently used are the organization's ability to fill key jobs with internal candidates rather than outside hires. At Dow Chemical, for example, an internal hire rate of 75 to 80 percent is considered to be a sign of success. Other quantitative assessments employed by the best practice organizations included:

❏ Ethnic and gender diversity in promotions

❏ Retention/attrition rates

❏ Positive job evaluations following promotion

Qualitative assessments tend to be based on issues such as the participants' transition experience into their new role, the quality of their preparation beforehand, reasons for attrition, and qualities of bosses in developmental assignments. Again, using Dow as an example, their qualitative assessment includes answers to such questions as:

❑ Was there a range of good choices for each position, as opposed to just one candidate?

❑ Did the transition go smoothly?

❑ Was the employee properly prepared for the position by her job experience, training, and developmental assignments?

❑ Did the candidate turn out to be the "right" person for the job, in both the long and short terms?

Each of the best practices organizations in the APQC study has developed its own unique structure for measuring and assessing the ongoing success of its succession management programs. Below are specific examples from the different organizations.

## Dow Chemical

At Dow, an *outside* hire into a functional-critical or corporate-critical role is considered to be failure in the internal development process. The company believes that its internal talent is extremely competitive with external talent. As a result, Dow uses the "hit rate" of the succession plan—whether the person placed in the open job was on the succession planning list or in the pool—as a measure of success. As noted above, a hit rate of 75 to 80 percent is considered to be a success. The remaining roles are generally filled by people identified as Future Leaders, but are not necessarily "ready now" candidates—they need developmental assignments.

Other means of assessment at Dow are a comparison of its Future Leaders' attrition rate with the company's global attrition rates (all management ranks). Dow's global attrition rate for 2002 was 5 percent overall, while for Future Leaders the attrition rate was only 1.5 percent. This higher retention rate indicates positive success on the part of the Future Leaders in terms of the opportunities they received for development.

The level of agreement among members of the Corporate Operating Board on Future Leader selection is an additional measure of success. If the members agree on the selected candidates, their agreement indicates satisfaction with the level of the candidates' professional development and preparation for the position. If there is disagreement, the sources of the disagreement are identified. More often than not, Dow has discovered that disagreements are based on a lack of data about the candidate or differing views surrounding results and accomplishments. If there is continued disagreement, a third-party or "neutral" executive is asked to work with the individual on task forces or other assignments. This executive then serves as an additional source of evaluation with the level of the candidate's professional development and preparation for the position.

As the process owners, members of the Corporate Operating Board debrief after every iteration of their succession planning meetings. An "action register" is kept, consisting of who will do what by when. For example, the action register may say that an executive was going to mentor a specific individual, provide a development experience for a person, or release a person. Such decisions are tracked to see if the action was carried out. In addition, Dow conducts benchmarking to assess the succession planning process, including a review of published, referenced literature reports from the Human Resources Institute, and reports from the Corporate Leadership Council during the design phases.

Finally, Dow conducted a longitudinal study in 2002 that tracked participants in the company's executive education program. It found that participants improved their strategic thinking, external focus, consumer orientation, and their global view based on multiple source assessments.

## Eli Lilly and Company

Lilly has two key succession management measurements (Figure 5-1)—the overall quantity of talent in its pipeline, and the number of succession plans where there are two or more "ready now" candidates. Both metrics play an important part in answering the question, "Do we have enough talent for both the near term and the long term?"

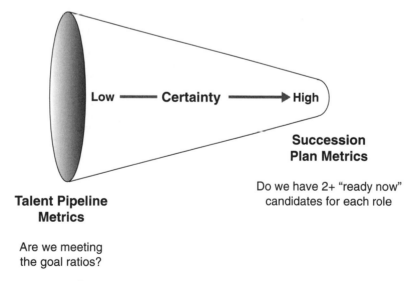

Figure 5-1. Lilly's two key succession management measurements.

Talent pipeline metrics look closely at the ratio between incumbents at a level and individuals with potential at that same level. There are specific goal ratios for each level of management (e.g., 3:1 for the director level). Additionally, both groups are segmented to specifically track diversity. Lilly tracks the percent of incumbents and potentials at each level for gender, race/ethnicity (U.S. only), geographic origin, and certain experiences (e.g., cross-functional assignments). Lilly believes diversity is a critical element of business success because if employees actually reflect the interests of customers, they are likely to make better decisions. They also purport that improvement of diversity of its "potentials" is a leading indicator of the diversity of its overall population.

The succession plan metrics help the company understand the readiness of the pipeline and where gaps exist. Lilly understands how many "ready now" candidates it has for its top 500 positions. Similarly, it also understands where there are no "ready now" candidates and uses that information as a work flow trigger for executive recruiting activities. Additionally, analysis is done to understand how "thin" the pipeline might be. Metrics are gathered to determine how many individuals are on more than three succession plans as "ready now" candidates.

A further benefit of more rigorous succession planning is that it becomes linked to employee development. Supervisors who place individuals up for candidacy for certain roles, either in the near term or long term, know that they must guide the development plans of those employees in ways that prepare them for those responsibilities.

These metrics are reported by the succession management team that leverages a single database for the entire company. Reporting to both the senior management team for Lilly and specifically HR occurs monthly and quarterly. A detailed annual review of the metrics occurs with those groups as well as with the board of directors.

## Sonoco

The company does not perform any statistical analysis on its succession planning process. Instead, human resources supports a functional measure of the system, asking, "Are we placing candidates in appropriate open positions, and are they successful in those positions?" When Sonoco implemented its succession planning process, HR asked division administrators for feedback on the new process. On average, divisions reported a 75 percent savings in time, compared to time spent in previous years. The division administrators expect that time to decrease even further as they become more familiar with the system. In addition, Sonoco has found that the performance/promotability matrix is 80 to 90 percent accurate in its predictions.

## Dell Computer

One of the primary metrics reviewed by the organization is bench strength. Each business unit is responsible for reporting the percentage of positions with a current successor and with identified successors. Additionally, Executive and Organization Development tracks movement and development of the Global Corporate Talent pool on a quarterly basis and reports the results to the Office of the Chair (OOC).

## PanCanadian

The company relied on more informal feedback sessions to assess effectiveness, for example, discussions about the number of high-potential employees who terminated their employment, readiness levels of individuals, and length of time key positions remained vacant. As an integral part of its succession management goals, PanCanadian promoted diversity awareness to ensure that bias did not negatively influence promotion decisions. While no specific numerical diversity targets were set, the company deployed a simple model with a wide variety of diversity categories for its succession discussions. It included the mental and occupational categories presented in Figure 5-2 and a secondary analysis, under the physical category, of gender and age.

The diversity framework was used to guide preliminary discussions that integrate diversity in the succession management process. The highlighted elements, such as age, education, and style, received attention via data gathering and dialogue. Consideration of these diversity factors helped PanCanadian monitor its achievement of succession planning goals.

## Bank of America

The succession planning process is measured in several ways. The first is by measuring the performance goals. Is each business achieving its talent goals? Even if it is currently meeting them, is it positioned to do so in the future? Does it have the leaders to achieve even greater results? Consequently, one measure tracked is, "Does each business unit have a top performer (achieving the right results ['the what'], the right way ['the how,' i.e., by living Bank of America leadership competencies and values]) in each of its critical business leadership roles?" If not, then the talent review discussion focuses on determining who will be moved into these roles.

A second measure tracked and monitored is the number of

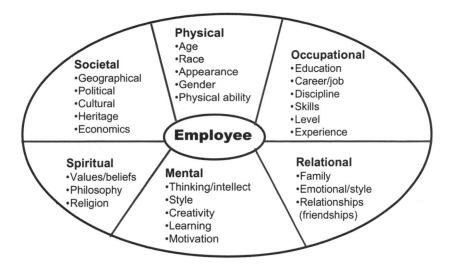

Figure 5-2. PanCanadian's diversity framework.

"ready now" replacement candidates for any one of the company's top fifty or so jobs. The goal is to have at least a 2:1 ratio of "ready now" replacements for each of these roles.

A third measure is diversity. Given the changing demographics of the bank's 27 million or so existing and future customers, it is a business imperative that Bank of America have the right diversity mix in its leadership ranks. Their objective is to ensure that associates mirror and outpace customers demographics. The bank looks forward some five years in terms of demographic trends to set its standards. At Bank of America, diversity is conceived in broad terms; race, gender, language skills, internal (promoted from within) versus external (hired from the outside) Bank of America and banking industry experience, and so on. All of these dimensions are tracked down to the individual business unit level.

What makes the measurement process work effectively is the integration that exists between talent planning/succession planning and the other management structures that hold people accountable. For example, the bank's annual planning processes include a rigorous and simultaneous assessment of the alignment between strategic, financial, risk, and organization/people planning. In many firms, the people part of the annual plan is at the tail end of the process and is dependent on what remains in the budget. In addition, each of the bank's executive's quarterly business performance review involves a discussion regarding progress made against annual talent planning commitments and results achieved because of those changes (both organization and individual people results). Metrics such as retention of top performers and leadership diversity mix in the key roles are also tracked and ultimately tied to an executive's compensation.

Different methods of evaluation and assessment work well in different organizations, depending on company culture, its talent needs, and business goals. The important factor is the use of a clear method of assessment to identify areas of success and areas that need improvement. A combination of qualitative and quantitative assessment methods yields a richer look at an organization's level of achievement in succession planning.

## Lessons for Long-Term Success

Despite the innovative processes exhibited by the best practice partners, they all have faced challenges in instituting the succession planning process and have learned lessons along the way. In addition to lessons learned, they have focused on the continuous improvement of their approaches. For example, at Dow, the business functions wanted to retain their own succession systems with all of their own candidate profiles and information. Over time, as the succession process matured and trust in it increased, the functions saw the need for one common IT system serving as a knowledge management system for all of the profiles and information across the company. This led to the creation of "LeaderDev," an IT tool that contains all of the profiles and input for the entire organization. The following section highlights the past challenges and future aspirations of this book's best practice organizations.

## Bank of America

The success of Bank of America's succession planning process is attributed to Ken Lewis, the CEO. He personally sets the annual agenda and focus for two-hour talent reviews with each of the top revenue-generating business executives as well as each key functional leader. More important, he holds his people account-able for the decisions made in these meetings through his man-agement routines as well as by maniacally checking up to ensure follow through and accountability on the part of executives. Mr. Lewis fundamentally believes that leaders do matter and having the right people in the right roles at the right time is a competi-tive advantage, ultimately making a difference in Bank of Ameri-ca's ability to deliver on customer, shareholder, and associate commitments.

Second, while the succession process is managed centrally (common templates, tools, rating scales, leadership competencies, analysis, etc.) through *corporate* personnel and executive develop-ment, each business unit and its respective executive teams are expected to own the process, the recommendations, the deci-sions, and the consequences related to the actions taken. Leeway is given to each business unit to customize the process and to tailor recommendations around current and future business issues and challenges.

Third, the success of the bank's succession planning process can be attributed to the fact that it is seen as an activity directly tied to achieving the company's growth projections and goals. All succession planning meetings and discussions start *and* end with the question, "How will the recommendations increase revenue, profits, customer satisfaction/delight, productivity, associate satisfaction, and shareholder value?"

Last, the business unit succession process and, more importantly, the CEO reviews are focused on *discussion* over form; *decisions* over considerations; and *simplicity* over pomp-and-circumstance. There was a time when a leader could walk into her review with the CEO with an entourage of support partners armed with large binders of materials and analysis. Today, the CEO manages these discussions in a much simpler way. He, along with the bank's top human resources and finance executives, meet with the senior line/function executives. They are armed with only three pages of materials outlining the information and recommendations that will drive the level of discussion, decisions, and commitments in the meetings.

## Dell Computer

The success of Dell's succession management process is directly attributed to the involvement of the Office of the Chair. The members of the OOC are visible and important drivers of the process. A second success factor is simplicity. Dell ensures that succession management information is easy to absorb and actionable by senior executives because its process balances structure and discipline with simplicity.

Dell plans improvements for its organizational human resources planning (OHRP) cycle on a yearly basis. Plans for the next cycle include (1) creating a user-friendly OHRP database that links to other human resource systems, (2) strengthening the conceptual linkages between OHRP and development activities, and (3) improving leadership forecasting processes.

## Dow Chemical

Dow also similarly believes that executive buy-in is critical for successful succession planning. The company stresses the need to keep the process simple and manageable while tying it into the strategic agenda at the executive level of the organization. In implementing a succession system, Dow cautions organizations not to expect significant change immediately. According to its experience, change takes time before it is readily accepted and then embraced. As with any system change, people need to see that the old way of approaching succession planning is unacceptable, that the new approach is owned by the top executives, and that the process is simple, straightforward, and not overengineered.

In addition, Dow recommends keeping the competency list short and refraining from asking managers to predict future succession planning needs more than a few years in advance. It also believes that global organizations should identify leaders and manage their development according to function rather than businesses. This is due to the fact that the company's businesses are so similar to one another. Many skills are not business specific but rather function specific. The succession challenge for Dow is therefore providing both experiences in multiple functions and in managing multiple functions. Moreover, the company's global organizational design does not readily offer "small" general management experiences for development. As a result, Dow is today searching to find ways to create similar developmental positions through subsidiaries and joint ventures.

Over the next few years, Dow plans to become even more focused on employee development. It aims to be more aggressive in its staffing strategies and in linking long-term staffing and development to business strategies. Dow's overarching goal is to keep its focus on empowering and enabling the total workforce rather than becoming preoccupied with managing only its Future Leaders. In 2002, Dow launched a corporate global *People Strategy*. It contains five key elements:

1. Attracting and retaining the talent needed to be successful

2. Having all employees focus on continuous learning

3. Having a performance excellence culture

4. Embracing diversity and inclusion

5. Having leadership at all levels and empowered teams

## Eli Lilly and Company

The elements that contribute to success at Lilly include making the process mandatory, overcommunicating to the appropriate people (the ones using the database), strong CEO and senior management involvement, integration with other HR processes, and a drive to make the process and tools as simple and understandable as possible. A key component in these goals is the use of an intranet Web site tailored to meet the specific needs of the process. This global tool helps to formulate metrics, manage knowledge, and fill open positions. "Off-the-shelf" software was investigated but was deemed to be more expensive and less functional than the custom alternative.

Two recommendations for success offered by Lilly are to implement *one* consistent and simple process, and *one* reliable technology solution—a database that works—for the enterprise. It is important to concentrate on creating one central, synchronized database. Lilly's achievements in succession management are also attributed to the organization's culture of valuing professional development. The associates at Lilly understand that passing up opportunities, hoarding information, or promoting the wrong people can be detrimental to an organization.

"I can't emphasize enough the value of having our process and tools being Web-based," comments Mark Ferrara, Lilly's director of Global Staffing. "Not only does this improve accuracy and allow global, real-time deployment, but perhaps most importantly, the tools are built as a response to our process. I believe many companies make the mistake of letting a software product drive their process, which inevitably causes complication and confusion."

## Sonoco

Similar to our other best practice companies, the following elements are critical for a successful succession planning system:

1. Senior management supports and uses the process (making it more than just an exercise).

2. It is simple and practical to use.

3. The design solves the organization's particular succession planning needs.

4. There is a serious commitment on management's part to applying the results.

One of the challenges faced by Sonoco, however, is keeping track of key people who do not operate in the main office in Hartsville, South Carolina. For divisions outside Hartsville, accessing and transferring files is currently time consuming, and HR has been searching for ways to improve remote access. A second challenge lies in having employees ready for promotion, which is one reason that the succession planning system is so important. A third challenge is that Sonoco tends to promote from within a functional area, so one of its goals is to promote individuals across divisions and functions with greater frequency. A final challenge is the need to revisit an individual's development plans and his progress throughout the year with greater consistency. There is a tendency for review to be a once-a-year event.

# Other Lessons for Success

In addition to the company-by-company lessons listed above, there were a variety of lessons that seemed to be recognized across the board. While the succession management process looks different in every organization, and while the methods for measuring success vary as well, there are certain characteristics of an effective program that are universal. These characteristics can serve as requirements for success or as yardsticks for the qualitative assessment of the program.

## Smooth Transitions

Having someone to step into an important vacancy is a critical measure of the effectiveness of succession management. We would argue, however, that helping that person make the transition in a positive manner with all the necessary skills and knowledge is as important and more challenging to execute. Each subsequent level of promotion is a move away from specialization and toward generalization, an emphasis on strategic over tactical thinking, an increased need for cross-functional knowledge, and an increased need for leadership skills. Even at the top levels, the move from general management to senior management or even partnership brings with it a whole new set of expectations. So world-class succession systems are not simply concerned about having found the "right" developmental opportunity for a candidate. They are as concerned about a successful transition into the new role and provide high levels of support to make it happen.

Organizations that fail to prepare employees for these transitions and to mentor them through the process risk losing, to one degree or another, their investment in that employee. The failure to meet this challenge can mean that all of the work of the prior stages of the succession management process are derailed. Organizations must realize that transitions usually involve the need for new skills and attitudes. Despite the best efforts of everyone concerned, employees who have been promoted may not be fully equipped for these changes. The best succession processes identify beforehand how a candidate might derail and seek out steps to prevent such outcomes. They also provide support partners. For example, at Dow, there are three individuals attending to an individual's transition: her coach or mentor, the respective Human Resources business partner, and the director of Executive Development, who also provides confidential executive coaching.

At Bank of America, Brian Fishel and Jim Shanley and their staffs are quite conscious about ensuring the success of newly promoted or hired senior executives. While all the due diligence possible goes into the identification, assessment, and selection process, leaders in new roles can still derail. It is vital therefore that there be structures in place that leave little to chance when it comes to derailment. Hence, the bank has created a unique discipline around retaining newly promoted and hired executives—a process called Executive On-Boarding. It involves a set of processes and people to ensure a high probability of success (see Figures 5-3, 5-4, and 5-5).

Every senior executive promoted or hired into one of the top 250 roles at the bank receives a written on-boarding plan their first day on the job. The plan is created by a combination of the corporate personnel executives and a leadership development manager assigned to the new manager's business unit. It lays out a roadmap for success over the first calendar year. The plan lays out key relationships to build, key information to learn, and key goals and deliverables expected over the first 90 days, 180 days, and so on. One element which was discovered to be particularly helpful is a 45–90 day key stakeholder review process which the leadership development/personnel executive assigned to the new executive conducts on the executive's behalf. It is a very simple

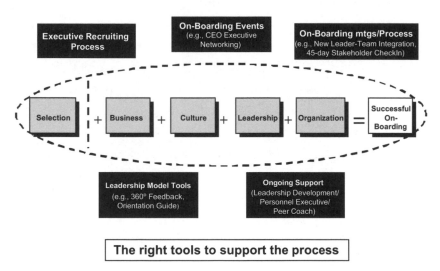

Figure 5-3. On-boarding tools and processes at Bank of America.

| Available Tools | Purpose | When |
|---|---|---|
| **New Leader On-Boarding Plan** | Organize and prioritize on-boarding events for new leaders | Week 1 |
| **Leadership Model Tools (e.g., Orientation Guide, Card Sort)** | Introduction to the Leadership Model; self-assessment | Week 1 |
| **Key Stakeholder Meetings** | Accelerate the development of stakeholder networks | Complete by Day 60 |
| **New Leader-Team Integration** | Accelerate the development of effective manager-team relationships | Days 60–90 |
| **New Peer Integration** | Accelerate the development of effective peer relationships | Days 60–90 |
| **45-Day Key Stakeholder Check-In** | Provide early feedback on strengths, development needs, and possible derailers. Develop an action plan to address these emerging issues | Days 45–90 |
| **KDL Executive Networking** | Create opportunities for networking with BAC leaders from other LOBs | Quarterly |
| **360° Feedback** | Provide feedback to the leader on BAC leadership competencies | After Day 180 |

Figure 5-4. Bank of America on-boarding tools.

and pragmatic process in which 10–15 key stakeholders are interviewed about the executive for 10 to 15 minutes apiece using the following questions:

❏ What are your early impressions of the executive's strengths?

❏ What are your early impressions on the executive's top two development needs that if gone unchecked could potentially prove to be fatal (i.e. derail their success)?

❏ What advice would you give the executive that will make her even more successful in his or her current role?

❏ What one thing do you personally need from the executive?

| Manager | **The key member of On-Boarding Team.** Makes the final hiring decision, clarifies performance expectations, guides the new leader's on-boarding process, shapes the on-boarding plan, and provides performance and development feedback and coaching to newly hired executive. |
|---|---|
| Senior Adviser | **Key stakeholder.** In a highly matrixed role, or when the support of a key stakeholder is critical to the new leader's success, it is often helpful to insert a senior adviser onto the on-boarding team. The initial role is to provide business perspectives and guidance, and can evolve into a mentoring role over time. |
| Peer Coach | **Peer of new leader.** Provides information and advice about the business, the team, and the role of the new leader. |
| Personnel Executive | **Primary Personnel Contact.** Lead personnel executive who supports the head of the business. Assists in the selection of the new leader. Takes the lead on clarifying roles/ responsibilities of the On-Boarding Team. Provides on-boarding guidance and support as needed. |
| LD Client Manager | **LD Support.** Involved in the selection of the new leader. Works with the hiring manager and the personnel executive to develop the on-boarding plan and review the plan with the executive. Facilitates 45-day stakeholder check-in (optional) and 360-degree survey feedback. Provides on-boarding guidance and support as needed. |
| Executive Development Consultant | **ED Process Monitor and Support.** Monitors the on-boarding process, consults on the development of on-boarding plans, maintains repository of plans, follows up with new leader, personnel executive, and LD client manager at month four. |

Figure 5-5. On-Boarding Team: Suggested roles and responsibilities at Bank of America.

The information collected from all the interviews is written up verbatim. That it is verbatim and anonymous is critical since it is seen as "unfiltered" information by the executives. The data are aggregated into a report that is given back to the new executive along with a summary and recommended development plan for the next nine months. The executive then is expected to share this report and plan directly with her boss.

Another unique process Bank of America uses is a forum called "CEO Executive Networking." This forum, sponsored directly by the CEO, who attends each session, is intended to help acculturate new leaders to the bank. It also provides a pragmatic means for the bank's current senior leaders to learn new ideas and best practices from the new executives. The sessions are run quarterly and entail a learning component, a sharing component, and a social component for purely networking purposes.

## The "Right" Developmental Assignments

As we discussed in Chapter 4, a successful process includes job assignments that properly prepare candidates for their new positions, as compared to the sink-or-swim approach that, while seemingly easier, may teach executives more about surviving and watching their backs than about leading. The developmental activities of best practice organizations include a wide variety of experiences, such as job assignments, education, action learning, and coaching.

Harvard professor Clayton M. Christensen suggests looking at business units or divisions as "schools," and the problems that confront managers in those business units as the "curriculum."[1] The skills that managers can be expected to possess and to lack are, therefore, heavily dependent on which "courses" they did and did not take as they attended the school of experience taught in their function or business unit. To assure success, Professor Christensen suggests that business units "can be profiled in this way, creating a road map of implicit developmental pathways and the resulting learning, positive and negative, that can be derived from its 'course work.'"[2]

Lilly, for example, segments its talent pipeline by types of potential. There are three types: technical (deep expertise in a functional area, but probably not aimed at people leadership roles), functional (expertise in a functional or geographic area as well as the ability to lead people), and cross-functional (strong learning agility and the ability to lead multiple functions or geographies). The company is careful to ensure that candidates are placed in the developmental roles for which they are best equipped to both learn and succeed—having learned the "hard way" by placing individuals in roles that required abilities for which they were not naturally predisposed.

## Meaningful Appraisals and Feedback

Honest communications and objective assessments are essential in order for management to specify what is required for a successful promotion. Multi-rater feedback (such as 360-degree feedback) is one way to avoid the bias of a single perspective, especially if it is supported by training for the users and follow-up assistance. Transparency about the developmental needs of an individual also requires a level of candor that is unusual in most organizations. Formal training in coaching techniques can help in this regard. For example, Lilly's Group Development Review (GDR) gives individuals a very clear understanding of both their strengths and weaknesses as viewed by a range of individuals. The feedback from this group is delivered by the individual supervisor with the intent of truly helping the individual understand how he might succeed.

## Appropriate Selection Criteria

As discussed in Chapter 3, a successful succession management system is dependent on the development of "competencies" for each job, giving everyone involved a clear picture of what types of skills, behavior, values, and attitudes are necessary for success.

In addition to making the process more efficient and consistent, it increases fairness to the employee by aiding diversity and eliminating certain biases. The challenge with competencies is that they represent not only today's needs but also should include needs required for the future. In addition to the competencies, all of the best practice organizations have a very strong focus on results and accomplishments.

## A Range of Good Choices

A working succession system results in having more than one good person available for a key job. For example, our best practice organizations targeted, at a minimum, two to three individuals for a position. Real success requires choices—sometimes painful ones—between two or more qualified people. Because the realities of the world make it uncertain when individuals are best prepared to move into a position, and because the needs of the organization change over time as a result of unforeseeable circumstances, the succession management process must be dynamic, with people constantly moving through different levels and on different tracks. Because of this variability, organizations like Dell and Lilly inevitably want to have choices when faced with openings in critical roles. That is why their process metrics are designed to help them understand any gaps in their talent pipeline.

As one might imagine, the positive outcomes associated with an effective succession planning process do not occur overnight. It takes several iterations and revisions of a succession initiative before it operates smoothly. For further detail on each of the best practice partners and how they accomplished their goals, refer to the case studies section, Appendix A.

# Conclusions About Assessment and Long-Term Success

1. Best-practice organizations develop methods of assessment to monitor the effectiveness of their succession planning process. These methods vary according to business goals and company culture. That said, the most effective systems clearly define the "success" of their processes according to the following outcomes: the successful placement of "ready now" candidates, retention and attrition rates, positive job evaluations following promotion, insider versus outsider hires, quality of preparation for the position, diversity objectives, the breadth of talent pools for positions, and the supply of developmental assignments. Perhaps the most important assessment source utilized by our benchmark firms was the feedback they received from the line managers who perform the actual assessment of key managers within the firm.

2. Recommendations for success from best practice organizations emphasized keeping the process simple and easy to use. As previously suggested, many of the changes made in succession processes were aimed at reducing the *time* required to manage the succession process. Success was also associated with effectively engaging technology to support the process in an easy-to-access, easy-to-use manner. Even a high technology firm like Dell reduced the emphasis on technology to make the system simpler for people in the field. Conversely, Sonoco has been able to link a number of software packages to make their system both robust and easy to use.

3. Aligning succession management with the overall business and corporate strategy is a condition of success. If this factor is in place, the most important ingredient for success is much easier to obtain: securing active senior level support for the process. No succession management system will be effective unless it is actively utilized and supported by top management. When the strategic advantages of succession management are clearly demonstrated, and there is responsiveness on the part of Human Resources to suggestions for improvement, the partnership between HR and top management rests on a solid foundation. That said, succession planning must also be an integral part of an overall human resource strategy.

4. Building an effective succession management system must be seen as a journey rather than a destination. All of our best practice partners talked about the continual changes they made to respond to suggestions from their clients. None of our respondents felt that they had a succession management system that would remain unchanged for any length of time. They were always listening to feedback and looking for ways to make the system serve senior management more successfully.

# Notes

1   Clayton M. Christensen, "Getting the Right Stuff in the Right Place at the Right Time," Harvard Business School Publication 9-601-054, July 17, 2001, p. 4.

2   Ibid.

# Chapter Six

# THE FUTURE OF SUCCESSION MANAGEMENT: BRIGHT LIGHTS, LOOMING CLOUDS

The transformation of succession management over the last ten years has been impressive. Driven in large part by the recognition that talented managers are a scarce resource, that the lifetime loyalty contract is in shambles, and that leadership development interventions can produce genuine long-term results, succession management today is a more dynamic and strategic process than ever before. Aided by technology, greater commitment on the part of executives and line managers, and streamlined systems and competency models, its future would appear to be highly promising.

That said, the ultimate effectiveness of any succession system depends on its ability to place talented individuals in "the right opportunity at the right moment," to retain that talent over the long term, and to produce a steady and sufficient supply of competent leaders, given existing and future demands facing the organization. In this chapter, we examine the trends that promise to further support our optimistic view of succession management's future. We also examine certain critical dilemmas that succession management will face—some of which are perennial problems and others that are products of the times.

# Bright Lights on the Horizon: Promising Trends for Succession Management

We believe that there are several critical trends that will further strengthen the transformation of succession management from a replacement tool to a development and leadership capability tool. These trends will also ensure that systems and processes continue to become more responsive and less bureaucratic. The most important include the migration of systems toward greater integration and simplification, technology platforms pushing succession to the "desktop," improvements of rigor in assessments, and more effective interventions supporting succession transitions for candidates. We examine these trends below.

## Greater Integration and Alignment

Succession planning will continue to become more integrated into the everyday life of organizations. It will move from a formal "annual event" and become part of the daily fabric of doing business. For example, regular staff meetings will include talent assessment discussions. This level of integration will occur partially because of a heightened awareness of the talent and leadership shortages that many organizations face at senior levels. It will also be facilitated by technological trends that integrate succession processes into the desktop personal computers of managers where a single icon can be clicked for immediate and widespread access.

Company-wide databases will demand uniform succession standards and processes throughout the organization. In addition, when organizations operate best practice succession systems, more and more managers will see the payoff for themselves in their own careers and for their functions and business units. Such positive experiences will transform how and when they think about succession. Perceptions will shift toward seeing succession as a part of every staffing decision.

Our research also indicates that all of the components of human resources management are being looked at, appropriately, as fully integrated, aligned systems, rather than as a set of disconnected activities. Corporate human resource development (HRD) is becoming the "hub" of these systems components, with primary operational responsibility and a partnership role with the executive team in shaping the strategy associated with each of the HR subsystems. One important shift underlies this change. It is the recognition that succession management cannot function effectively without an understanding of the strategic direction of the firm. The same holds true for management development and education initiatives. Historically, "silos" between human resources functions in different business units or functional lines kept one another from knowing what was happening in related functions.

This lack of communication and coordination is costly in the contemporary world of hypercompetition and is virtually unknown in our best practice firms. For any strategy to be successful, it must be communicated throughout the organization. Armed with information about where the firm is headed, astute human resources managers can help prepare qualified leaders to steer the corporate ship of state. Therefore, we will see savvy senior HR leaders design succession initiatives through corporate center "hubs" that will provide consistent standards and processes across all functions and lines of business. These "hubs" will coordinate developmental resources from training to coaching so that they are fully integrated into succession planning processes, rather than "siloed" off into separate HR functions or in business units and functions.

## Technology Moves Succession Planning to the Desktop

The succession planning group at Lilly has a simple expression to describe how managers need to experience the group's succession tools on their desktops—"Be like Amazon." This mindset is being realized by simple, user-friendly, Web-based succession tools that make succession planning feel less like another planning event and more like a commonsense weekly or even daily activity.

To increase access to and use of succession planning, our best practice organizations continue to turn to technology as a critical facilitator of the process. Most of these organizations today rely on Web-based succession planning systems so that it is an easy link from anyone's personal computer. By running the process online and integrating various software packages, best practice partners have been able to ensure *continuous* access to data and to encourage employees to take ownership of their own development plans through their own "desktops."

For example, Lilly's succession management system is fully

available on the company's intranet, twenty-four hours a day, seven days a week. Lilly operates SAP and Oracle databases hidden behind a fully customized succession management Web site. All employees are responsible for updating their personal information and resumes on the intranet. The resumes outline their career history, educational background, skills and strengths, and career scenarios they envision for their future. As a result, HR and the succession management team can instantly assess an employee's current level, potential level, experience, and development plans.

The Lilly succession management Web site also acts as a querying and reporting tool. HR can request specific information on incumbents, and the site quickly retrieves the information. When data are requested, the results are automatically downloaded to an MS Excel spreadsheet for easy viewing and customization. The resulting names of individuals are returned with a hyperlink, so that the succession management team can pull up the individual's online resume, a development plan, and the level of readiness for a move. In addition, the system allows HR to download summary metric reports that show real-time data for all the talent pipelines. With the capability to search for multiple criteria, Lilly can view any segment of the organization in one query.

Technology is also fostering greater transparency in succession management. At Dow, for example, the Job Announcement System posts openings online for positions below the top 800. In addition, a Web tool includes career opportunity maps that detail the sequence of jobs one can expect in a function or line of business. In some firms, compensation ranges are even shown by levels and by positions on the company. Therefore, technology not only facilitates greater transparency in the succession process but also ensures that planning is a far more pleasant process by making it less time consuming, simpler, and more flexible.

Interestingly, the highest technology firm among our benchmark firms, Dell Computer, reported that it had actually cut back
on the use of complex technology in certain succession management applications because its push for speed and simplicity led to
the conclusion that less complex, simpler applications were most
effective.

## Increased Rigor in Assessments

While it will never be possible to fully escape the subjectivity in
candidate assessments for succession, great progress has been
made toward more objective assessments. The primary contributor to this trend has been 360-degree survey feedback. As its use
expands, we will witness a broader array of raters such as secre-
taries, administrative support staff, and internal and external
customers. More importantly, best practice organizations will increase their efforts at training line managers and executives to
perform more objective assessments when providing 360-degree
feedback. Corporate HRD will become involved in training business line HR staff in how to run succession discussions with line
managers, with a strong emphasis on reducing subjectivity. For
example, staff will be taught how to listen for subjective comments in succession discussions and to explore in depth the thinking or feelings behind them. They will target circumstances where
managers prefer mirror images of their own style or approach. HR
staff will help assessors reflect on such biases.

# The Looming Clouds in Succession's Future

At the same time that we see important advances in succession
management, we do feel that there are a set of both new and

perennial dilemmas that will continue to limit the upside potential of succession management systems. Among the most important of these are insufficient supplies of developmental opportunities, generational resistance to certain assignments, inconsistencies in selection criteria and rewards, shortcomings in competency models, and limits on 360-degree feedback's potential as an assessment tool. Each of these issues is explored below.

## Finding a Sufficient Supply of Developmental Opportunities

One challenge facing a number of organizations will be supply problems with developmental opportunities for more senior roles. The problem is likely to be most pronounced at the general manager level. The positions usually feeding into this role are functional roles—for example, a vice president of marketing becomes the business unit head. Functional roles do not adequately prepare individuals for the cross-functional demands and enterprise perspectives demanded by the general manager position. In companies organized primarily along functional lines, the problem is particularly pronounced.

Global corporations that have moved away from a more decentralized organization built around country managers to one organized around global lines of business face a similar dilemma. Country manager roles tend to be excellent developmental grounds, since they often involve responsibility for multiple functions and have both an internal organizational and a market-facing responsibility. Trends at Dow, for example, illustrate this dilemma. Under their old organizational structure, some sixty countries had country manager roles that served as training grounds for general management talent. Today, these positions no longer exist. In their place are thirty global lines of business built around functional specialties. In addition, fifteen or twenty years ago, a manager might hold a country manager role at an age ranging from the late thirties to the mid-forties. Today, the average age for individuals heading the global lines of business is the mid-forties to the early fifties. So not only is the age increasing, but the number of developmental opportunities has been halved.

Increasingly, organizations will have to search more proactively for and create opportunities that provide general management experiences and do so at an earlier stage in a manager's career. Possibilities could include small joint ventures or new internal enterprises. Cross-functional and enterprise experiences might also be developed by lateral moves across functions and business units. For example, Dow recently increased the background assignments for any individual who is to be considered for a senior management position. Potential top executives are expected to have assignments that include both line and staff positions, domestic and international jobs, functional variety, and positions that deal with the public and regulatory agencies. By requiring this variety of experiences, managers can expect to receive assignments that are essentially lateral moves rather than always looking to the next position in their functional specialty.

## Generational Resistance to Certain Opportunities

A major challenge facing succession initiatives will be generational differences. Younger people may prove far less inclined to accept positions overseas or ones that require relocation in general. The current generation of retiring executives and managers is the last generation in which a majority of married couples had a single working spouse. Today's workplace generations are mainly dual career couples. Spouses are far more reluctant to be "trailing" or "in-tow" partners.

In addition, they are having children later in life. Their children's schooling years now often occur during their parents' peak career years—the forties and fifties. Developmental assignments and promotions must increasingly weigh the career and family options of both the manager and their spouse or partner. This limits the variety of assignments that are acceptable to the newer workforce generations. International assignments will be seen as particularly difficult to accept, since the persons' partners may not be able to find job opportunities comparable to their current one. In addition to the dual careers dilemma, Generations X and Y have witnessed the greatest surge in divorced parents in history. Not wishing such a fate for themselves, these generations are more concerned about achieving a greater balance between work and their personal lives. We may discover that they are far less willing than prior generations to say "yes" to promotions and assignments that demand long hours or extended periods of travel and separation from their families. If this proves to be the case, succession will become a more complicated issue. There may be shortages in the supply of those wanting to become senior executives. At the very least, organizations may find that the developmental assignments of old (an international opportunity or a turnaround assignment) may not be as attractive to younger generations of managers. In turn, we may need to become more innovative in terms of finding and designing assignments that do not demand relocation and long work hours, yet provide significant developmental opportunity.

## Inconsistencies in Selection Criteria and Rewards

One of the great challenges facing organizations in very dynamic environments will be inherent conflicts in selection criteria. In other words, do we select from the culture and requirements of today or in light of the culture and requirements we want for our future? This problem will be most acute for succession systems that cascade multiple levels below the executive suite. In these cases, succession systems are attempting to develop talent over the long term. In using uniform competency models across the numerous levels, the emphasis tends to be on rewarding behaviors that meet current or near-term needs of the organization. Yet the more junior managers in the system may not be promoted to general manager or executive roles for eight or ten years. Shouldn't succession systems be preparing these managers using a different set of competencies—a set that the organization believes will be required of executives in the next decade? The issue is a complicated one with no easy answers. It is clear from our research that a single competency model is the preferred approach because of needs for uniform system standards and simplicity.

Having two sets of competencies—one for existing needs and one for future needs—adds greater complexity and may raise questions of equity. Second, it is extremely difficult to know what will be required of executives in a decade. A set of future-oriented competencies is likely to be an exercise in speculation. That said, the lesson is that selection criteria must be continually revisited by the CEOs, their executive team, and the senior HR staff. It is not uncommon for succession criteria to become entrenched and over time to lose their relevance. Executives who are driving a major cultural or strategic change will certainly need to revise the existing selection criteria to reflect the new capabilities demanded by their agenda. The new generations of succession systems are designed to be far more responsive and strategic, given their greater engagement of system owners, their very simplicity, and ease of use. For this very reason, how we select and develop candidates must weigh the emerging needs facing the organization. One solution for some organizations will be to create new streams of assignments for junior managers to prepare talent cadres for capabilities and mindsets anticipated for five to ten years in the future.

## Competency Models—A Flawed Foundation for Development?

As we have noted throughout this book, competencies are an integral part of today's succession management systems. Yet competencies have their own important shortcomings. Since the majority of succession systems are built around these models, it is critical that we understand their flaws and the implications for development and succession practices.

> *An Intellectual Exercise.* Because of the rigorous research that is often involved in creating a competency model, some critics believe that the practice is often used to make "frustrated academics" in human resources assignments feel good about the "intellectual rigor" associated with these programs rather than their practical value to the firm. In a recent biography, Louis Gerstner Jr., who was chairman and CEO of IBM from 1993 until 2002, describes his experience with his firm's use of a competency model to drive changes in leadership behavior within the company. Using a set of eleven competencies (cus-

tomer insight, breakthrough thinking, drive to achieve, team leadership, straight talk, teamwork, decisiveness, building organizational capability, coaching, personal dedication, and passion for the business), training and evaluation were designed to reinforce these behaviors with the aim of producing a new culture at IBM. While Gerstner did indeed witness changes in behavior and focus as an outcome, he remained concerned that the process remained predominately an intellectual exercise.[1]

One major contributor to the limited impact of competencies was that IBM managers were still measured and compensated according to the old cultural behaviors. So metrics and rewards did not change to reinforce the new competencies. In addition, Gerstner concluded that there were simply too many competencies. In the end, he settled on only three—win, execute, and team. Each was defined with a few details. So while competencies played a role in developing a new generation of leaders at IBM, the model was *extremely* simple and had to be reinforced by changes in rewards and performance metrics. The more sophisticated model had very limited impact.

*Questionable Foundations.* Morgan McCall and George Hollenbeck, two experts on leadership development, take an even stronger stand on the limited utility of competences. They argue that competency models are largely ineffective as a foundation for developing leadership—especially at the executive level. They challenge the underlying assumption behind competency models: an effective executive leader is the sum of a set of "pieces" or competencies. The logic of these models therefore follows that if we develop each competency to the point of mastery one after the other, the executive will emerge as a successful leader. Yet as Hollenbeck and McCall point out, there are a myriad of ways of accomplishing an executive's jobs: "No two CEOs do the same things much less in the same ways, or have the same competencies. This conclusion is not only obvious on its face, it is evident when we observe outstanding leaders, whether military officers, heads of states, or CEOs—one cannot but be struck by the differences rather than the similarities in their makeup."[2]

In other words, to argue that executive jobs can be universally defined according to seven, nine, or eleven behavioral dimensions is grossly oversimplifying a very complex role. The very complexity of an executive position at the same time allows for multiple ways of doing the job and multiple forms of talents: ". . . [for example] a person may compensate for a lack of some skills (e.g., make up for a lack of knowledge in finance by drawing effectively on the knowledge of others), acquire missing skills (e.g., learn enough finance to get by), substitute something else for the skill (e.g., outsource), or change the job so that the skills are not so crucial (e.g., split off the financial component)."[3] So, at best, there is a "loose coupling" between the results an executive achieves along with the means to those results and any specific set of behaviors and competences.

Hollenbeck and McCall argue that the focus of developmental needs must move from behavioral models to "strategic demands." The first task is for senior leaders to define the strategy of the business and from there to identify the leadership challenges implied by these objectives. Experiences would then be identified which provided sufficient preparation for managers to meet such strategic challenges. Succession management processes would begin by focusing on the essential question: What types of jobs, special assignments, bosses, and education are needed to build the leadership capability to successfully achieve our business strategy? These "experiences" would be identified and safeguarded by the senior team as essential to the succession management process.

*Historical Bias.* The original competency studies were conducted by trying to determine what traits or behaviors (competencies) were found in managers who were viewed as
outstanding compared to those who were less successful. The
belief was that by hiring people with those traits or behaviors
or developing those unique competencies of the most effective
leaders in an organization, overall corporate performance
would improve. Unfortunately, as we noted earlier, the characteristics that helped current leaders succeed may not be appropriate for the new leaders required for the evolving
challenges of tomorrow. A few insightful organizations have
begun trying to identify the characteristics or competencies
that their future leaders will require. While not lending itself
to the kind of research methodology associated with historical
competencies, we believe that the future focus is essential for
competencies to be valuable for their users.

While we share Hollenbeck and McCall's belief that strategic needs should indeed shape succession management, we
do feel that competency models have a place. As we have
pointed out many times, these models do need to be simple
to be effective. As importantly, many of these models focus
on the interpersonal dimensions of effective management behavior. If solely strategic needs were to drive succession decisions, we would be concerned that many of the softer
influences and interpersonal skills would be overlooked.

# 360-Degree Feedback as an Administrative Requirement: Weakening a Powerful Development Tool?

Another foundational element of today's succession management
systems is multi-rater or 360-degree feedback. Increasingly, these

survey tools provide important insights into the developmental needs of a manager and therefore have become a vital source of information when it comes to succession planning. They are of course based on competency models, and so they are subject to the same dilemmas raised in the prior section. There is, however, an additional problem. What happens to 360-degree feedback information when it becomes part of the candidates' records for assessing their capabilities for promotions and assignments—in other words, when their feedback results are "quasi-public" instead of solely under the candidates' ownership, as is the case with many succession systems?[4]

We do know that feedback has a special status if the person receiving feedback owns it entirely, i.e., the results are confidential. Research suggests that information gains in value merely by being owned.[5] Researchers at the Center for Creative Leadership, for example, argue that, in order to change and develop, individuals need to feel psychologically safe and to "own" their evaluations.[6] Therefore, if the goal is truly development, ownership of 360-degree data by the recipient is crucial. When 360-degree data is used for administrative purposes like succession management, the data become the property of the organization, not the individual.

It is quite reasonable to expect that simply the labeling of the purpose of 360-degree data collection as either *personal development* or as *succession management* will activate different motivations. This will generate differences in the behavior of those receiving the feedback. There is empirical evidence, for example, that raters change their ratings when 360-degree feedback becomes a performance evaluation tool in place of a development tool.[7] More than 70 percent of managers in one study admitted to having inflated or deflated evaluations in order to send a signal to protect a colleague or to shock a poor performer.[8]

How we frame the purpose of survey feedback therefore has an impact on participants' attitudes toward 360-degree assessment. For example, when the purpose is purely development (rather than for succession management), individuals receiving the feedback are likely to be more motivated to look for accurate feedback with an aim to make decisions about enhancing the effectiveness of their behavior. When the purpose is succession management, they may be more inclined to seek favorable feedback and to increase their ratings by managing impressions. Managers may focus only on what needs to be done to get higher ratings. In other words, the focus of their attention will shift from behavior change, which requires serious effort, to carefully contrived actions designed to impress or please those who are rating them. Managers will seek *favorable* feedback over *accurate* feedback. For example, they may selectively demonstrate more timely responses or provide greater favors to those peers who are likely to be chosen as their raters.

In addition, research suggests that seeking knowledge about ourselves is driven by three different motives—the appraisal, self-enhancement, and consistency motives.[9] The *appraisal motive* reflects the need of an individual for accurate feedback from others. People are curious how others perceive their abilities, traits, etc. The *self-enhancement motive* encourages people to seek favorable information about themselves. It suggests that we have strong preferences to learn that we are good. The *consistency motive* is a quest for evidence that confirms what people already know about themselves. It is reflected in a tendency to reject contrary evidence and to be resistant to change.

Common sense would suggest that accurate information is more useful than favorable or confirming information, especially when it comes to development. However, research shows that self-enhancement is the strongest motive when we pursue knowledge about ourselves. This is followed by consistency, and, unfortunately, the appraisal motive comes last when we process information referring to ourselves.[10] These findings point out that there is a strong and deeply rooted self-enhancement orientation in our behavior. When the goal of 360-degree assessment is for succession decisions, we can expect that the self-enhancement motive will be further strengthened because it often leads to rewards in terms of promotions and special assignments. In this case, thinking well of oneself and inflating one's view of oneself will become even more desired. The impact that self-deception processes have on our behavior is well documented. People try to minimize the time spent on processing critical feedback.[11] They may selectively forget negative feedback.[12] To make matters worse, the organization itself often ends up with invalid data. The only mitigating factor may involve receiving accurate information from people, such as supervisors, whose perceptions matter for real consequences. So we need to exercise great caution as we move 360-degree feedback data into serving an administrative or assessment role in succession management. We may actually end up limiting its usefulness as a tool for developmental feedback.

# The Essentials for Successful Succession

In closing this chapter, we want to address two important remaining issues, one related to the implementation of a new succession system, and the other related to the organizational mindset required for genuine success of any and all succession management processes.

## Implementing a New System

*Top Management Champions*: To reinvent an existing system or to launch a succession management system for the first time within your organization, it is absolutely critical that buy-in begin with the executive team of the overall organization. The best practice partners in this study as well as the research sponsors agreed that the success of succession management hinges on a deep commitment from the executive officers and most importantly from the CEO. These individuals must become highly engaged and feel that they are the actual owners of the system. The HR champions for a succession system must therefore convincingly argue that succession will pay long-term, handsome dividends. The champions must talk the language of the executive team emphasizing the fact that the organization's strategic needs will drive the system. The emphasis must be on getting their perspective on what is important, how it will help them to achieve their future business goals.

As part of the championing process, the executive team and line managers must be assured that the system will not be allowed to become bureaucratic nor become too complicated or time-consuming. This is typically a great concern for the business unit leaders. To borrow a term from the world of software, it must be experienced as "user friendly." Early on, business and functional heads need to be engaged to make certain that there is widespread agreement, buy-in, and more importantly, that there is a consistent, uniform system throughout the organization.

*A Powerful Coordinating HR Hub*: Corporate human resources must play the role of the "coordinating hub" so that each business unit or function does not create conflicting systems or models. As importantly, by placing control of succession management at corporate, the message is reinforced that talent is the property of the entire organization not a specific line of business or function. The activities of the hub include designing the overarching competency models, facilitating talent review forums with the CEO, training functional and business unit HR staff to implement and facilitate succession processes in their units, establishing the technology platforms for succession planning across the organization, providing oversight of the system performance, and ensuring continual process improvements.

*Identifying Linchpin Positions*: After commitment is gained across the organization, the next step is for the corporate HR group to begin by identifying key or linchpin positions across the organization. These positions are critical to the success of the organization, involve important development opportunities, are difficult to fill, and require coordination with other parts of the organization. These might include regional management, key functional assignments, general management in a small business unit, or a critical staff assignment. From there, an assessment of what these jobs offer in terms of development opportunities needs to be determined. It is also critical at this stage to decide exactly how many levels of the hierarchy will be involved in the process.

*Realistic Talent Assessment*: Once the linchpin positions are identified, the next step is to begin a talent review process for these positions. Individual functional and business unit senior level managers review with their direct bosses (the functional and line of business heads) the status of all their direct reports and their own talent assessments. This typically includes the individual's performance to date, some type of 360-degree feedback, and a development plan. It can be more sophisticated (see our descriptions in earlier chapters) but generally it is best to begin simply.

This review must involve "multiple points of view." This could be achieved through 360-degree assessments but this type of data must be complemented. At one firm we studied, the company launched their talent review process by asking the manager or sponsor of a nominated high potential to identify three individuals who were at least one level above the candidate and knew the individual well. They typically brought a cross-functional perspective on that individual. A 90-minute dialogue with all three present was conducted to assess the career potential of that candidate. In other firms, the review process involves HR succession specialists interviewing subordinates and peers about the candidate's capabilities. The critical point is to get a well balanced set of perspectives beyond the candidate's immediate supervisor. Very often if somebody is managing upwards well, but not managing their peer and direct report relationships well, the gap is very evident in a multiple points of view process.

Out of the talent review should come first and second step career options or "next steps" for each candidate. These should clarify what are likely to be the next two or three job moves for this person within the next one-to-two and all the way out to five years. In addition, the review focuses specifically on talent in the linchpin positions and on those about to advance into those roles.

The conclusions and recommendations of these assessments are then rolled up together and presented by the senior-most line manager or functional head to articulate the overall bench strength vis-à-vis linchpin positions and development needs for candidates within their part of the organization. This presentation includes a review of high potentials for linchpin roles, how many are well placed, how many are ready for developmental assignments in the near term, and where are staffing gaps retention vulnerabilities, and shortages of developmental assignments for linchpin roles. The presentation is made before the CEO, executive team, and senior HR officers.

*Continual Process Improvement*: What we have been describing so far is the ideal set of first steps towards implementing a successful succession system. Along the way, HR officers and succession specialists need to be canvassing both the sponsors and the candidates to determine how to further improve the process—what can be simplified further, what needs to become more user-friendly, what are overlooked dimensions, and so on. These systems are only effective when their owners and users find them highly responsive to their needs and when the tools and processes are easy to use and provide reliable and current information. In the early years of a new system, owners and users are likely to find any number of shortcomings. It is therefore imperative that the HR officers and staff responsible for succession management be actively engaged in a focus on continual improvements.

## The Foundations for Genuine Success

While the war for talent may seem passé today, the foundation on which a truly effective succession management rests is a mindset that talent is king—in other words, a belief that talent *directly* impacts the performance of the organization. This belief sets up a mandate for the organization—to get and keep talent. It depends on a deep comfort with differentiating performance between individuals and in turn a corporate culture in which candor is more highly valued than politeness or tolerance for average or poor performance. Jim Shanley of Bank of America explained in a 2003 interview:

> You need a strong succession process, but it is not the process that really makes the difference. You have to have a talent mindset. But a talent mindset requires that your executives feel comfortable talking about who are their A players. Do they talk frequently about these people and are they comfortable differentiating them from others? You need to know who your best people are and that you are moving them in logical ways. You also need know who your bottom performers are so that you can move them out to give stretch assignments to new people. The focus must be on the top performers and the bottom. I see a lot of companies wasting time dissecting the 50 to 70 percent of the people in the middle. In addition, if the executive in charge or the executive team does not have a meritocracy or talent muscle-building philosophy, does not have a belief that talent directly impacts the business, and is not willing to demand candor, then you may have a succession process but its results will be shallow.

The focus on the bottom performers at Bank of America stems from observations that such individuals, when situated in critical roles, produce a significant number of dysfunctional outcomes for the organization. For example, they block opportunities for others to advance into their roles. They often do not develop subordinates adequately, and they tend to produce work environments of low morale, low productivity, and low customer satisfaction. In turn, they may actually drive away the top performers beneath them. Top performers want good bosses and great challenges at a fast pace. Poor performers act against all three.

Shanley at Bank of America has found it particularly helpful to think of succession against the backdrop of a set of forces that must be in place for genuine success. One is that the organization must believe in and act on a fundamental value proposition, which is to get and keep *great* talent. This must be combined with a talent mindset that emanates from the top. This mindset is built on a belief that talent directly impacts the business and that executives can successfully differentiate the "A players" from others. The value proposition and mindset, however, must be supported by an organizational culture that encourages candor and risk-taking at the executive level. Executives must be willing to talk candidly and frequently about people. They must not only feel comfortable differentiating between people but in placing top performers in stretch assignments. They themselves must be held accountable for developing people and for giving insightful feedback. In addition, the culture must value meritocracy and talent muscle building where the performance bar is continually raised. Finally, these dimensions must be further complemented by formal leadership development processes where there is line management accountability, simple and rigorous action-oriented talent review processes, joint ownership between the executives and management of the development of the top tier of management, robust processes for recruiting, assimilation, performance management, feedback, and coaching, and education and development. Without all of these elements in place, succession systems will never realize their full potential.

In our roles as researchers and consultants, we unfortunately see too many organizations in which time and energy are spent largely on one element of formal leadership development processes. Yet it is clear to us that in environments that are not keenly focused on getting and keeping great people, where key senior leaders do not have a genuine talent mindset, and where candor and risk-taking are undervalued, even the best succession management processes will remain underutilized.

# Notes

1    Louis V. Gerstner, *Who Says Elephants Can't Dance? Inside IBM's Historic Turnaround* (New York: HarperCollins Publishers, 2002), p. 210.

2    George P. Hollenbeck and Morgan W. McCall, "Competence, Not Competencies: Making Global Executive Development Work," Working Paper, Center for Effective Organizations (University of Southern California, 2002), pp. 8–9.

3    Ibid., p. 17.

4    G. Toegel and J. A. Conger, "360-Degree Feedback: Time for Reinvention," *Academy of Management Learning and Education Journal* (2003), forthcoming.

5    D. Kahneman, J. Knetsch, and R. Thaler, "Experimental Tests of the Endowment Effect and the Coase Theorem," *Journal of Political Economy* 98 (1990): 1325–48.

6    Maxine Dalton, "When the Purpose of Using Multi-Rater Feedback Is Behavior Change," in David Bracken, Maxine Dalton, Robert Jako, Cynthia McCauley, and Victoria Pollman, eds., *Should 360-Degree Feedback Be Used Only for Developmental Purposes?* (Center for Creative Leadership: Greensboro, N.C., 1997), pp. 1–6.

7    David Waldman, Leanne Atwater, and David Antonioni, "Has 360 Feedback Gone Amok?," *The Academy of Management Executives*, 12(2) (1998): 86–94.

8    C. Longenecker and D. Ludwig, "Ethical Dilemmas in Performance Appraisals Revisited," *Journal of Business Ethics* 9 (1990): 961–969.

9    R. Baumeister, "The Self," in D. Gilbert, S. Fiske, and G. Lindzey, eds., *The Handbook of Social Psychology*, vol. 1 (Boston, Mass.: McGraw-Hill, 1998), pp. 680–740.

10   C. Sedikides, "Assessment, Enhancement, and Verification Determinants of the Self-Evaluation Process," *Journal of Personality and Social Psychology* 65 (1993): 317–38.

11   R. Baumeister and K. Cairns, "Repression and Self-Presentation: When Audiences Interfere with Self-Deceptive Strategies," *Journal of Personality and Social Psychology* 62 (1992): 851–62.

12   W. Crary, "Reactions to Incongruent Self-Experiences," *Journal of Consulting Psychology* 30 (1996): 246–52.

Appendix A

# Detailed Case Descriptions

In thinking about how readers would want to access the information generated by our research, we decided to emphasize the topics contained in the preceding chapters. In those chapters, we attempted to extract key examples of how the benchmark companies approached or dealt with the issues under consideration. We realized, however, that some readers might become fascinated with the approach of a particular firm and want to know more about their approach to succession management. We do not recommend that anyone attempt to adopt the "ABC" approach on a wholesale basis. Still, we hope that most readers will enjoy reading, in some detail, about how Dell, Dow, Lilly, Sonoco, and Pan-

Canadian manage the growth of their company's future leaders. In the following pages, we present the edited reports generated by our site visits and survey data with each of the best practice partners. Since Bank of America was not part of the original APQC panel, it is not included in this appendix.

## Dell Computer Company
Industry: Computer systems
Headquarters: Round Rock, Texas
Revenues: $35 billion (estimated 2003)
Employees: 35,400 (2003)
Web Page: www.dell.com

Headquartered in Round Rock, Texas, Dell Computer Company is one of the world's top PC makers and premier suppliers of Internet technology. Led by founder Michael Dell, the longest-tenured CEO of any major U.S. computer company, the firm sells hardware and markets third-party software and peripherals. Products include PCs (approximately 55 percent of sales), servers, storage products, and customized services. Government entities, large businesses, and educational institutions purchase nearly 60 percent of Dell's systems.

Dell is second worldwide in market share and consistently the leader in liquidity, profitability, and growth among major computer systems companies. With approximately 35,000 employees, Dell had estimated revenues of $35 billion in 2003. Ingrained in Dell's organizational development processes for six years, succession management includes the following three elements: (1) review leadership needs and key talent, (2) identify gaps between needs and talent, and (3) develop plans to close those gaps.

Each business unit leader is required to participate in an annual cycle of planning and review that results in succession plans and individual development plans for their direct reports. Each business unit has the option to implement the succession management process to greater depth.

This case study focuses on Dell's core succession management process for the business unit leaders and their direct reports and its connection to executive development. Topics include:

❑ Roles

❑ Processes and tools

❑ Leadership development

❑ Measurement

# Introduction

The backdrop of Dell's succession management and leadership development practices is the Dell business model, which is characterized by direct relationships with customers, suppliers, and employees. By customizing products to meet individual needs and vertically integrating distribution and manufacturing functions, Dell dramatically reduces time and costs. Because Dell changes and grows at a rapid rate, the succession management process accelerates the development and movement of leaders.

# Roles

The office of the chairman (OOC) is the champion and final audience to the succession management process. The OOC consists of CEO Michael Dell and copresidents and COOs. On an annual basis, all business unit leaders present, in a standardized and structured format, their succession plans and their leadership development to the OOC. The OOC then probes deeper into those decisions, identifies gaps, and advises on action plans.

The OOC also participates in quarterly meetings where business heads discuss possible transfers among the business units. The quarterly review process is designed to increase development through movement among the business units. The business unit leaders are ultimately accountable for developing the leadership potential within their units by using the customized tools and processes provided by human resources.

The Executive and Organization Development group is part of the corporate human resources department and consists of six individuals responsible for designing and rolling out organization and leadership development processes. Primarily, one person in that group handles the succession management process and tools. Human resources departments within the business units are responsible for supporting the process. They use tools provided by the corporate Executive and Organization Development group to customize the succession management process.

## Evolution of Succession Management

The succession management process has evolved over the last six years to better meet the needs of the corporation and its business units. The three distinct phases of development are:

1. Organization and Management Development Review

2. Organization and Human Resource Planning phase one

3. Organization and Human Resource Planning phase two

The Organization and Management Development Review was Dell's first attempt at organized succession planning. A rigorous and manual process, the review was in place for two years. However, the review was complicated and made it difficult to isolate the most critical information for building leadership. In pursuit of a succession management process that was more focused and easier to use, the Organization and Human Resource Planning (OHRP) process was launched. In this new process, Dell reduced the number of management layers that required a succession plan, reduced the number of individuals reviewed, and shifted the focus to aligning organizational strategies with changes to leadership development. To support the process, the Executive and Organization Development group teamed with internal IT resources to develop a global, Web-based software application that entered, stored, and analyzed the succession management data.

## Organization Planning

Feedback on the OHRP process indicated that the business units valued the focused content, but the software application was more of a barrier than a facilitator.

The software application was thorough and automatically generated the presentation materials required for the OOC review. The consistency of data allowed for easy presentation and provided a complete database of information on leaders that could be searched and queried. However, the software left no flexibility for the business units to tailor the process to better meet their unique needs. This inflexibility, combined with problems experienced with the speed and usability of the software application, led to the next phase of the OHRP process.

# Processes and Tools—Organization and Human Resources Planning

After gathering extensive feedback from business leaders and human resources, the Executive and Organization Development group modified the succession management process so that it was more business focused, simpler, and less time consuming. While allowing flexibility and customization for the business units, the alignment of plans for the growth of the organization and of the leadership pool remains the focus of the process. The OHRP process includes:

- ❑ Review of leadership needs

- ❑ Review of leadership talent

- ❑ Identification of gaps between needs and talent

- ❑ Development of plans to close those gaps

- ❑ Executive review (the OOC presentation)

- ❑ Ongoing development, movement, and measurement

## Development Movement Measurement

The primary tool used to support the OHRP process is an MS Excel workbook. Each element of the planning process has a corresponding MS Excel template that is used to organize and present the results to the OOC.

# Leadership Needs Assessment

Leadership needs assessment focuses on forecasting how many leaders Dell will need to drive growth, as well as the qualities that are required of those leaders. The qualities are defined in a Dell competency model, and future requirements for successful leadership are embedded within the model. Because of Dell's priority to adjust to the quickly changing market through segmentation and reorganization, it has been difficult to predict the number of leaders needed and at what levels. Two templates, a current organization chart and a future organization chart, are provided to the business units to help with needs assessment. The current organization chart defines leadership presently in place and locates gaps in leadership. The future organization chart displays what the organization will need to look like in twelve months in order to handle growth and change in the markets. Business units pull data from their strategic objectives, business plans, and current business results to define their organizational needs.

# Talent Assessment

As part of the succession management process, each direct report to the business unit leader is reviewed according to the criteria in the individual profile. The key data reviewed includes:

- ❑ Basic biographical data
- ❑ Career history
- ❑ Career interests
- ❑ Potential jobs in the short and medium term

- ❑ Competency strengths and development opportunities

- ❑ High-potential identification

- ❑ "Scaling call" (which refers to an individual's ability to handle a bigger job)

- ❑ Review of developmental actions from the last twelve months

- ❑ Preview of developmental actions for the next twelve months

Although the method for collecting data varies by business unit, the ideal scenario is when the manager and the individual discuss the profile information and agree on the ratings.

# High Potentials

High-potential talent is identified at the corporate level—Global Corporate Talent—and the business unit level (functional high potentials). Anyone specified as Global Corporate Talent (GCT) is also profiled and reviewed for the OOC. The GCT pool consists of individuals with the capability to run significant portions of a function or business and who can leverage skills or experience on a global basis. Dell invests a significant amount of resources and senior management time to the GCT pool, which is made up of fewer than 100 individuals in the company. As mentioned above, the business units also have functional high-potential programs that identify talent deeper within their organizational structures. The functional high potentials are generally not reviewed in the OOC presentations.

Scaling calls are used to identify an individual's ability to grow into a higher-level job or scale with the growth of his or her current job. Individuals are rated on the following five-point scale:

1. Promotable

2. Develop in place

3. Contribute in place (struggling but manager willing to invest more time)

4. Manage out of position

5. Too new to call

## Assessment Methods

The ultimate assessment of an individual's competencies, high-potential status, and scaling call is the result of multiple sources of data. Some standard sources of data used across the company are an annual performance plan and appraisal, individual development plans, career discussions, and the results of 360-degree feedback. Some business units use additional sources of data, such as the results of assessment centers and a development interview process. The business unit leaders employ the completed profiles to describe their leadership talent to the OOC. The business unit leaders own the data.

## Gap Planning

Once the business units assess the leadership needs and identify leadership availability, development actions are specified for each individual in the individual profile. Individuals that are "ready now," "ready in one year," or "ready in two to three years" are identified.

## OOC Presentation

The completed plans (in the form of the completed templates described above) are presented by the business unit leaders to the OOC on an annual basis. The business unit leaders discuss their organization charts, organization changes, succession plans, and details of the individual leaders in their group. In addition, the business unit leaders may use the last portion of the presentation to discuss whatever other issues and plans they feel are relevant to building their bench strength.

The OOC uses this opportunity to gain a line of sight to the top leaders in the organization, as well as advise on structure, movement, and developmental actions for the business unit leader's direct reports. It is the first step in establishing accountability for leadership development among the business unit leaders. The commitments made and the results of those commitments are reviewed on a quarterly basis during each business unit's operations review.

## Leadership Development

After the OOC review, each business unit leader is responsible for carrying out the developmental actions specified in the individual profiles for his or her direct reports and any Global Corporate Talent from the unit. The development actions are highly individualized to meet the person's specific needs and can include many types of activities, such as:

- ❏ Executive education

- ❏ 360-degree feedback

- ❏ Mentoring

- ❏ Coaching

- ❏ Assessment centers

- ❏ Project assignments

- ❏ Job assignments

- ❏ Cross-organizational movements

In addition to development efforts, the OOC invests time grooming and retaining individuals in the Global Corporate Talent pool. The OOC is actively involved in the career and skill development of this pool, particularly through cross-organizational movement of the individuals in the pool.

# Dell Competency Model

Dell's development programs (e.g., executive education and 360-degree feedback) are based on the Dell competency model. The competency model was created through analysis of 360-degree feedback data, performance appraisals, derailment studies, strategic organizational requirements, and benchmarking data. These competencies were shared among excellent performing leaders and identified core success factors across business units and specific functions.

Five competencies were evaluated as entry-level requirements for leadership positions:

1. Functional/technical skills

2. Integrity and trust

3. Intellectual horsepower

4. Business acumen

5. Command skills

The following nine additional competencies were identified as success factors for leaders:

1. Priority setting

2. Problem solving

3. Drive for results

4. Building effective teams

5. Developing direct reports

6. Customer focus

7. Organization agility

8. Learning on the fly

9. Dealing with ambiguity

Applied in relevant human resources tools and processes, these competencies are integrated into a recently adopted career development model that assists individuals in developing their careers through four stages. The first stage is for new hires to understand how to approach Dell's direct-selling business model. The second and third stages focus on learning how to contribute independently and collaboratively through leadership. The last stage centers on gaining organizational leadership.

# Executive Education

Executive education at Dell is driven by feedback and targeted to specific needs of the individual. Competency-based, executive education is a blended model of e-learning and leader-led curriculum. Course titles include:

- ❑ Executive On-Boarding

- ❑ Influencing with the Dell Business Model

- ❑ Update Dell's Position in the High-Tech Industry

- ❑ Executive Level Communications at Dell

- ❑ Strategic Leadership at Dell

- ❑ Analyzing and Presenting Effective Business Proposals at Dell

- ❑ Executive Level Presentations at Dell

- ❑ Strategic Management at Dell

- ❑ Strategic Management Business Simulation

Other methods for executive development are through online interaction. Dell Direct is an intranet site that allows executives to participate in conversation groups and online interviews. Executives also have access to book signings, literature, courses, orientation materials, and speaker slides. The site is accessible to all executives.

Dell's 360-degree feedback program is a survey process that collects detailed, behavior-based data on an individual's job behavior from his or her boss(es), peers, direct reports, and customers. Throughout the program, individuals identify gaps in their behavior (i.e., assess their manager's perception) and then develop steps to improve performance. The data is owned by the individual and used for developmental purposes only. The individual is responsible for sharing his or her key learnings with the manager and jointly developing a plan to address them.

## Cross-Organization Movement

Movement among the business units has historically been a challenge at Dell. The organization has grown very quickly, which has led business units to bring in their talent and develop it as quickly and efficiently as possible. Cross-organizational staffing processes have tended to be too slow to meet the business needs.

In the current OHRP cycle, the Executive and Organization Development Group is experimenting with a new process to facilitate cross-organizational movement. Profiles of top-executive talent feed into the creation of talent pools. The Executive and Organization Development group places individuals into talent pools based on their level within the organization, readiness for promotion, needed experience, and competency strengths. The group then creates position pools (of anticipated vacancies) based on job characteristics. The potential moves within the organization are mapped, and business units can use the information to initiate cross-function moves.

The purpose of talent pools and position pools is to increase the visibility of executive talent among the business units and to provide a forum for making decisions about talent movement. The OOC and the corporate Executive and Organization Development group are primarily concerned with facilitating and tracking cross-organizational movement at this level in the organization. Promotions to director and vice president positions are approved by the OOC on a quarterly and biannual basis.

To further pursue cross-organizational movement, Dell is currently implementing a pilot, biannual executive talent movement meeting among interested business units with similar competency requirements.

# Measurement

By consolidating the data in the succession plans and individual profiles, Executive and Organization Development creates an executive database. When all business units have completed their annual presentations to the OOC, Executive and Organization Development analyzes the company-wide data to identify strengths and opportunities among the leadership bench.

One of the primary metrics reviewed is bench strength. Each business unit is responsible for reporting the percentage of positions with a current successor and the percentage of positions with successors in the pipeline. In addition, Executive and Organization Development tracks movement and development of the Global Corporate Talent pool on a quarterly basis and reports the results to the OOC. Planned improvements for the next OHRP cycle include: (1) creating a user-friendly OHRP database that links to other human resource systems, (2) strengthening the conceptual linkages between OHRP and development activities, and (3) improving leadership forecasting processes.

## Success Factors

The success of Dell's succession management process is due to the involvement of the Office of the Chair. The members of the OOC are visible and important drivers of the process. The OOC participates in the annual review, as well as quarterly operations reviews in which leadership development issues are discussed. Senior executives also invest significant time in the Global Corporate Talent pool. A final factor for success is simplicity. With a process that balances structure and simplicity, Dell ensures that succession management information is easy to absorb and actionable by senior executives.

### Dow Chemical Company
Industry: Chemicals
Headquarters: Midland, Mich.
Revenues: $28 billion (estimated 2003)
Employees: 50,000 (2003)
Web Page: www.dow.com

Dow Chemical is a world leader in the production of plastics, chemicals, hydrocarbons, herbicides, and pesticides. After Dupont, Dow Chemical is the second-largest chemical company in the United States. It recently acquired Union Carbide, making Dow the second largest chemical company in the world and the largest chemical company in sales in 2002. The innovative science and technology company provides many essential consumer markets with chemical, plastic, and agricultural products. Forty percent of its sales comes from performance plastics, such as adhesives, sealants, and coatings. Dow Chemical operates 123 plants in 32 countries. With the acquisition of Union Carbide, Dow now has approximately 50,000 employees throughout the world, with a physical presence in 63 countries. They serve customers in 170 companies.

Prior to 1993, Dow was organized around a traditional, multinational model with great emphasis on geographical management. In hindsight, this organizational structure led to excessive internal focus, competition for resources, and insufficient focus on competitors and customers. In order to increase the external focus, Dow decided to transform itself into a more global business. It implemented global work stations, computer architecture, and software standards so that all geographic areas could communicate. Dow installed 29,000 new computers in three months and began eliminating the barriers to sharing information and communicating across the globe. As a result, geography became less of a factor in decision making, and Dow was able to focus more on business and less on geographic differences. Dow instituted a strategic blueprint in 1993 that involved competitive standards for each global business unit. It focused on four critical areas for improving business: setting the competitive standard business by business, value, growth, productivity, and culture. In addition, Dow moved to a culture of greater employee responsibility rather than corporate paternalism. Another significant change was the move from an emphasis on measuring sales to measuring economic profits. This strategy is still used today.

Along with the move to a more global business structure and elimination of much geographic infrastructure came extensive work, process engineering, and a 23 percent reduction in the global workforce. This reorganization resulted in six layers of management as opposed to twelve or even fourteen in some areas. New emphasis was placed on operating self-directed work teams and eliminating levels of management.

This transition to global work processes also affected the human resource function. In the "old" Dow, one human resources (HR) person served 70 employees. Now one HR person serves 110 employees. Human resources at Dow became more effective and efficient by implementing HR global resource, or learning centers, and by providing services online. Occasionally, Dow receives requests from locations for a local or business-customized services HR person, but overall, the company is very pleased with the efficiency. Customer satisfaction surveys demonstrate first quartile satisfaction from both employees and managers. With the movement to a more global organization, Dow's Executive Committee introduced People Success in 1996. People Success is an integrated HR system based on eight global competencies:

1. Initiative

2. Innovation

3. Interpersonal effectiveness

4. Leadership

5. Learning

6. Market focus

7. Teamwork

8. Value creation

For the first time, human resources operated around one set of dimensions. In the past, different sets of competencies were used in hiring, evaluating, and compensating employees. Each global division had its separate leadership plans that rolled up to the corporate group. Dow's succession management strategy now links directly to the corporate strategy and addresses issues such as leadership at all levels; development and education opportunities; diversity; attraction and recruitment; and reward, recognition, and retention. The high level of corporate structure and support for People Success empowered the work force concerning HR issues. That said, each Dow function has a second set of competencies that are function-specific and are used in conjunction with the eight global competencies.

# Deploying a Succession Management Program

Succession planning at Dow is defined as the global process for identifying corporate critical roles and preparing successors for those roles. The process design team includes the vice president of human resources, the CEO, and the Workforce Planning Strategic Center. Together, the Workforce Planning Strategic Center and HR business partners facilitate the process, and the Corporate Operating Board owns it. The Corporate Operating Board, which includes the CEO and his fourteen direct reports, oversees the succession management process from the executive level. Within the HR department, the global director of workforce planning is the focal point for succession management. An internal design team benchmarks and improves the process. The Corporate Operating Board spends three to five days reviewing the talent pool and succession planning every January and commits ten full days to the process throughout the year.

Succession planning is a continuous process throughout the year. Every January, the Corporate Operating Board reviews the outcomes of the future leader process and discusses future leaders who may need cross-business unit experience. Compensation plans for the top seventy positions and options packages are also reviewed. In March, May, September, and November, the Corporate Operating Board reviews the progress of the global functions and businesses over the past year by studying the implementation of development plans and the nomination of new future leaders, and discussing which jobs will need a succession plan.

## Identifying the Talent Pool

Dow's working definition and management of the succession planning process has been in place since 1997. Dow defines a future leader as an employee who excels in all the global and functional competencies as well as in a subset of the global competencies reflected in the hybrid competency/experience, called "international effectiveness." Management notices his or her accelerated development and intervenes in his or her career planning to ensure that Dow provides the individual with the development opportunities needed.

Through employee development, Dow prepares candidates to assume leadership positions. Dow attempts to identify 5 percent of the professional or managerial population as future leaders and provide parity in gender, race, and global citizenship in the selection.

## Succession Planning Tools

Dow does not use a rating or ranking-based performance appraisal or assessment. Individual development plans and performance on goals are the key mechanisms through which management identifies high-potential employees and an employee's need for further development opportunities. In addition, Dow provides developmental 360-degree feedback for all its employees on a twelve- to thirty-six month voluntary schedule, although it is mandatory for future leaders every two years. In addition to the individual development plans, Dow utilizes a management scorecard that includes employee attitude scores on a global employee opinion and action survey. While some pilots and experiments have been conducted in the past with assessment centers, Dow historically has not used these systems; however, since the merger with Union Carbide, Dow is piloting a Development Center as a way to enhance team performance at the level of global business teams.

# Four Stages of Professional Development

The four stages of professional development at Dow are called *acquiring, applying, leveraging,* and *visioning.* The acquiring stage occurs early in an employee's career, when he or she is obtaining new knowledge. Movement through the acquiring stage is a planned progression, leading to the applying stage. In the applying stage, the employee begins to utilize his or her new training, experience, and skills. This is the level attained by all employees who stay with the organization and is the level from which most employees retire.

The leveraging and visioning stages encompass the top 3,000 employees in the corporation. The leveraging stage requires that the employee have impact beyond the work group and local site. These are true boundary-spanning roles. An executive cohort of the visioning stage is called the *global leader job family* and encompasses the top 250 leaders in the corporation. For compensation purposes, there are two salary bands within each applying, leveraging, and visioning stage (below global leader level). Future leaders are identified from the four professional development stages according to the following percentages:

- ❏ 40 percent of the global leader job family
- ❏ 15 percent of the visioning population below global leader
- ❏ 9 percent of the leveraging population
- ❏ 4 percent of the applying population
- ❏ 1 percent of the acquiring population

## Talent Pools and Talent Lists

The process used to select succession nominees varies by level and type of job. For roles with similar competencies, Dow identifies a pool of "ready now" nominees. A talent pool ensures there are enough candidates for each job and minimizes the reappearance of the same candidates on each list. Dow uses the guideline of attrition rate multiplied by three to estimate the number of candidates that should be in the talent pool. For unique roles, such as CFO, controller, and VP of R&D, the Corporate Operating Board uses a short list of three or four ready now candidates.

## Online Job Announcement System

Job openings are posted online on the Job Announcement System (JAS) for all jobs below the top 800 positions. Interested internal candidates apply and are interviewed based on structured, behavioral experience interviews designed around the global and functional competency requirements of the job. Due to this open market system, Dow does not conduct formal succession planning for positions covered by the Job Announcement System. Employees can self-nominate for an announced job, and a hiring manager can identify a preferred candidate where one exists and must state so on the Job Announcement System.

The Job Announcement System creates open access for employees to most jobs. It lists all jobs online in the appropriate language for the location of the position. If an employee cannot understand the language that the job description is written in, then he or she should not apply to work in that country. The Job Announcement System empowers employees to take control of their own careers. Dow's perspective is that people know what opportunities exist externally, so they, similarly, should be aware of and have access to internal opportunities.

# Succession Planning for Higher-Level Positions

The top 250 positions are broken down into categories of business- or function-critical roles and corporate-critical roles. Business- or function-critical roles compose approximately 200 jobs, where the role is not subject to redesign in the event the incumbent leaves and management continuity is considered a business or technical imperative. Business and functional leaders on the Corporate Operating Board own them with review by the full team. A corporate-critical role is a role not subject to redesign if the incumbent leaves and orderly management succession is deemed a fiduciary responsibility.

The organization's top seventy jobs are considered to be corporate critical. Succession planning for these positions is owned by the Corporate Operating Board, with the CEO as the second level review. For higher-level positions that fall between the scope of the Job Announcement System and function-critical designation, the functions (businesses for the commercial roles) identify talent through the future leader process for review in the annual people reviews. At these meetings, the Corporate Operating Board reviews the professional development of the future leaders from the previous year and nominees for the upcoming year's development investments. The Corporate Operating Board considers the demographics and representation from the four different professional development stages and discusses future leaders who are in need of a role change. It is then up to the functional leaders on the Corporate Operating Board and their staff to fill the higher-level jobs. Succession planning happens for most of these roles; however, the process is not monitored at a corporate level, but rather within the Functional Leadership Teams.

A future leader is defined as an employee who demonstrates accelerated development in the critical competencies. Two indicators of future leaders at Dow are:

1. They learn jobs faster than peers.

2. They impact the organization faster than their peers.

In order to assess employee performance and identify high-potential individuals, five of the global competencies are used with a hybrid of competency and experience called *international effectiveness*. To be considered, a future leader must be developmentally precocious on several of these competencies and fully meet the requirements of the functional competencies and other

global competencies. The global competencies were developed internally, and the future leader subset was derived from profiling
the corporate-critical roles.

## Competencies to Identify Future Leaders

In order to be selected, future leaders must have potential and
perform at a level above their current position on selected competencies. Employee performance and potential is evaluated according to the eight aforementioned competencies. In addition to the
eight global competencies, each business group also uses another
set of competencies that are function or business specific. Based
on a combination of the global competencies and the functional
competencies, jobs are profiled and employees can access the resulting competency profile, which details the role requirements
and expectations.

Employees can be identified as future leaders as early as two
to three years with the organization, especially if they are hired
with prior experience. In identifying future leaders, particularly
in higher-level roles, Dow emphasizes the importance of working
effectively outside the person's country of origin. Having lived
outside their home country is not a prerequisite for employees'
advancement into top roles, but currently, 80 percent of Dow's
top executives have multinational work experience. Dow believes
that this experience is necessary in a truly global company. The
process to identify future leaders is functionally driven. The individual must succeed in his or her function first, and then the
employee is encouraged to seek cross-functional experience or
cross-business and technology experience.

Although employee development plans are encouraged but

not mandatory for all employees, written development plans are required of future leaders. The plan must be submitted and reviewed by the Corporate Operating Board when the employee is nominated by his or her leader. Development and implementation of the development plan is the responsibility of the employee's leadership, but other members of the Corporate Operating Board may be engaged to create significant cross-business, cross-function, or cross-geography opportunities. Future leaders typically move three times as fast as others, so their role change is frequently a promotion. Talent outside the company is seldom considered in Dow's succession planning. External hires are required to prove their status as a future leader regardless of their position of hire or background. Dow consistently promotes from within, and it fills only half a percent of executive positions from outside the organization. Reasons for hiring externally could include a lapse in the development program, the need for a significant change in the direction of a business or function, or a specific need such as diversity.

## Engaging Future Leaders

After a future leader has been identified, management intervenes in the employee's career development by providing a developmental experience such as international exposure or cross-business functional exposure. All employees have access to mentoring, internal and external development classes, and the job announcement system to seek professional development opportunities; however, some executive development programs are restricted to future leaders. It is difficult for the employee to get involved in many special assignments without management intervention. Examples of executive development opportunities at Dow include:

❑ Mentoring

❑ Coaching

❑ Internal programs

❑ University-based programs

❑ Web-based programs

❑ Job assignments

❑ Special assignments

❑ Action learning

Although performance appraisals are not conducted, Dow makes available 360-degree feedback for all employees to hone in on areas of employee development. In addition, the required employee development plans for future leaders address identified competency or experience gaps. The individual's leaders or extensive online resources provide developmental suggestions, such as participating in a university class or in coaching or mentoring activities, or committing to a task force assignment or transferring to another company location. The individual then chooses from the approved set of developmental options. Dow has identified various universities across the country, which employees can attend, that specialize in areas such as entrepreneurialism, technology, and international affairs.

New employees are assigned a mentor, at which point the mentoring process moves forward informally. Experienced hires are also given a mentor in order to feel more comfortable at Dow. Coaching is an external service for employees in top positions. Internal development programs include more than sixty tools and classes available online. Dow Learning Centers worldwide have classroom activities and some select university programs at graduate business-school level. The university-based programs are typically one- to four-week programs at institutions such as the University of Michigan, Indiana University, Babson, IMD, IN-SEAD, and the Thunderbird Institute. Dow uses consortium programs where several companies cooperate in the academic program. Dow generally has no impact on the university program's curriculum, but it may provide input for the consortium curriculum.

Other methods to engage future leaders include special assignments like task forces or action learning exercises. Action learning exercises provide participants with the opportunity to study a particular topic area and present their findings to others. Frequently, participants are assigned an idea to improve business results, processes, or relationships, and they analyze the topic. In the development of future leaders, emphasis is on competency development, rather than development for a specific job, because there is no guarantee that a given job will exist in the future. In summary, Dow uses a variety of methods to engage future leaders and assist in their professional development. Dow does not report its list of future leaders or high-potential successors to the rest of the organization.

# Web-Based Applications

Dow extensively utilizes Web-based functions to support people, people leaders, and development, but it does not manage the succession management process virtually. People Success, Dow's comprehensive, competency-based human resource system, has a "finder" that is a Web-based portal to information on all aspects of the systems. It is organized into four principle sections:

1. Performance expectations (competencies by job level)

2. Employee development (training classes and programs)

3. Compensation (pay planning and promotions)

4. Employment opportunities (job announcement and application system)

People Success delivers HR services 24 hours a day, seven days
a week. As a supplement to the Job Announcement System discussed earlier, People Success includes career opportunity maps
that detail the sequence of jobs that feed or follow sample jobs.
Previously, Dow depicted these career paths on a career ladder,
but the use of a map represents a career journey rather than an
upward climb on a ladder.

The People Success system represents a significant shift from
past thinking, when employee compensation was extremely secre-
tive. Business leaders wanted to create an open market in which
all employees have access to HR information. People Success is
the umbrella that houses all HR functions.

Another Web-based tool is Learn@dow.now, an externally
developed online learning and training program. More than 600
courses are offered online at Learn@dow.now. Dow reports that
14,000 online courses were completed per week by employees.

Examples of training courses available on the site include
safety training, a required course for executives on respect and
responsibility training (addresses diversity and how to treat others), and compensation planning tools (that addresses geographic
differences in pay structure). In some instances, managers are no-
tified when employees do not pass the course. Initially, Dow
planned for PeopleSoft to manage the future leader and succession planning processes; however, the applications were too lim-

ited. Instead, Dow has recently implemented an internally developed MS Access database with HTML interface to track development plans. Although this capability exists, Dow focuses on the discussion component of development planning rather than on tracking the plans and system administration.

## Monitoring and Assessing the Program

At Dow, an outside hire for a function-critical or corporate-critical role is an indication of a problem or failure with internal development. Dow believes that its internal talent is extremely competitive with external talent. As a result, Dow studies the hit rate of the succession plan—whether the person placed in the open job was on the list or pool—as a measure of success. The hit rate yields a 75 to 80 percent success rate and is the primary measure of success for the succession-planning program. The balance of the roles is generally filled by people identified as future leaders, but not necessarily as a ready now candidate for the open position.

An internal longitudinal study that tracked participants in Dow's executive education program found that participants reportedly improved their strategic thinking, external focus, consumer orientation, and global view. The participants also demonstrated an increase in both compensation and performance compared to their colleagues who did not participate in the program.

Other means of assessment are the global attrition rates compared to future leader attrition rates. Dow's global attrition rate for 2002 was 5 percent overall, while for future leaders the attrition rate was only 1.5 percent. This higher retention rate indicates satisfaction on the part of the future leaders in their opportunities for development. The level of agreement on future leader selection among members of the Corporate Operating Board is an additional measure of success. If the members agree on the selected candidates, their agreement indicates satisfaction with the level of the candidates' professional development and preparation for the position. As the process owners, members of the Corporate Operating Board debrief after every iteration of their succession planning meetings.

Dow's use of benchmarking to assess the succession planning process includes a review of published, referenced literature reports from the Human Resources Institute and reports from the Corporate Leadership Council during the design phases. Dow does not prioritize benchmarking in succession planning because this system works in its culture, and the results may vary within other corporate cultures.

# Critical Success Factors and Lessons Learned

Dow emphasizes the importance of executive buy-in for a successful succession planning process. It also stresses the need to keep the process simple and manageable and to build it into the agenda at the executive level of the organization. Dow cautions organizations not to expect significant change immediately; according to its experience, change takes time before it is readily accepted and then embraced. Dow recommends keeping the competency list short and refraining from asking managers to predict future succession planning needs more than a couple of years in advance.

Finally, Dow suggests that global organizations identify leaders and manage their development according to function rather than businesses. Factors that classify Dow's approach to succession management as innovative include the Web-based functions People Success and Learn@dow.now, discussed above. In addition, succession planning is approached from two different perspectives. It is not only addressed according to critical job basis (i.e., which successors are in line for a given position), but it is also addressed from the employee development side (i.e., which employees are ready for a new challenge). These two approaches meld together at the senior management level because the top fifteen people in the company drive the succession management process.

# Dow's Future Goals and Objectives

Dow feels it is about half way on its journey to implement fully and realize the potential value from the current succession planning process. Over the next few years, Dow intends to become even more focused on employee development. It plans to increase the management of its future leaders more as corporate assets than as assets in a given department, business, or function. There are also plans to be more aggressive in its staffing strategies and linking long-term staffing and development to business strategy. In addition, Dow hopes to improve its methods of documentation and its use of knowledge management in the succession planning process. Finally, Dow's overarching goal is to keep its focus on empowering and enabling the total workforce rather than becoming overly preoccupied with managing only its future leaders.

## Eli Lilly and Company
Industry: Pharmaceutical
Headquarters: Indianapolis, Ind.
Revenues: $11.5 billion (estimated 2003)
Employees: 43,000 (2003)
Web Page: www.lilly.com

Indianapolis-based Eli Lilly and Company is an innovation-driven pharmaceutical corporation whose product portfolio includes the areas of neuroscience, endocrine disorders, cancer, cardiovascular diseases, gene regulation, bone, and inflammation, as well as animal health products. It is best known for developing Prozac, the world's first antidepressant of its kind. The company is expanding its drug pipeline, boasting approximately 40 potential products. Lilly employs over 43,000 people worldwide (about 14,000 in its Indianapolis headquarters) and markets its medicines in 146 countries. It has major research and development facilities in 9 countries and conducts clinical trials in more than 60 countries.

# Definition of Succession Management

Eli Lilly and Company's definition of succession management is to put the right person in the right position at the right time. Talent and position assessment play a vital role in the development of the succession plan. Some major questions posed are:

❑ What is the employee's level and type of potential?

❑ How prepared is the employee for advancement?

❑ Who should be in the corporate pools?

❑ What are the employee's career plans?

❑ Is the employee a "flight" risk?

❑ What positions are critical?

❑ When will we need a successor for each key position?

# Organizational Structure

Lilly's organizational chart starts with the CEO, who is followed by vice presidents, executive directors, directors, managers, and supervisors. The first level of management at Lilly is a supervisor. Succession management has been part of the Lilly corporate culture for many years and extends deeply into the organization. The succession management process is facilitated by human resources (HR) but is driven by the CEO and the senior vice president of human resources. Line management is responsible for the outcomes, but HR owns the process and has a seat at the table. Recognizing high-potential employees and fostering talent was carried out by a talent assessment program until 2000. At that point, the bar was raised when HR moved from talent assessment to rigorous succession management.

Senior management recognized the increasing importance of succession management and the need to overhaul the existing system for greater effectiveness, simplicity, and consistency. Lilly maintained its existing HR structure to carry out its goals. The reengineered approach leveraged new definitions, new terminology, and a Web-based system. The succession management team was responsible for carrying out these new goals.

Lilly's succession management team facilitates professional development planning, identifies employee potential, formulates succession metrics, develops tools, and manages employee data through an intranet site. The team uses tools that create consistency in the information gathered to ensure that the appropriate employees are selected for open positions. As a result of the changes in 2000, the team now focuses on the content gathered rather than the process of gathering information. For example, in past succession management meetings, the first 45 minutes focused on processes (e.g., on definitions and information). Now Lilly maintains a focus on content validity by providing consistent templates, definitions, and tools that drive a single database of employee information.

Lilly reports a 6 percent corporate turnover rate, and rarely goes outside to find senior-level talent. Succession management focuses primarily on the executive levels and evaluates all employees in exempt level positions within three years of hire.

## Behaviors (Competencies)

The CEO identified seven core competencies against which all employees are measured. Specific functions advocate additional behaviors that vary by specific management levels and are assessed, reevaluated, and updated frequently. The behaviors are kept current and future focused, based on the changing needs of the business.

## Talent Pools

Lilly has three focused, corporate talent pools. The first two pools, the general manger and product team leader pools, are composed of individuals who have cross-functional talent and can lead multiple disciplines. The third pool is for individuals who need an international assignment in order to develop leadership skills and behaviors. Nominated individuals must have at least director potential and must be supported by their home function.

## Managing Succession on the Intranet

Lilly's succession management system is available on the intranet for company-wide HR use. Nardoni and Associates powered the first generation of software in the mid-1990s; but given the corporate goal of rigorous succession management, Lilly needed more room to store and query data. Lilly now runs an SAP and Oracle database hidden behind a fully customized succession management Web site in a global or national environment. The database was conceived in-house and farmed out to a local software developer for fine-tuning. Lilly will soon further leverage its Web-based system to manage its succession plans.

Currently, only HR has access to the database information, but each employee at Lilly has important input responsibilities. Each must create a corporate resume and development plan that contains his or her picture (optional), positions held, past jobs, skills, abilities, aspirations, strengths, and job expertise. The development plan is entered into the database after a formal performance review and supervisor approval. Each employee is responsible for his or her own performance management, and each employee's performance management results are added to his or her profile and used for development plans and career planning (see below for more on development plans and career planning). The resume and the development plan allow decision makers to compare strengths (resume) and opportunities (development plan).

The succession management group anticipates many advantages in allowing employees to view and update their personal information on the Web. (Resume information is available, but not the results of performance management.) Most importantly, the information on the intranet is updated by the employee in real time to ensure that the information is correct. Encouraging and empowering each employee to create and update his or her own profile creates buy-in for the system. Simultaneously, line HR and the succession management team can assess an employee's status, potential experience, and development plans.

## Querying and Reporting

The site also acts as a querying and reporting tool. Human resources can request specific information on incumbents (e.g., females with director potential within the finance department or vice presidents with cross-functional skills and expertise). The tool was built on "the Amazon model." When an individual goes to Amazon.com, he or she types in search criteria and, with the click of a button, a list of books or movies is instantly displayed. Lilly's system works in the same fashion. When data is requested, the system downloads the results to an MS Excel spreadsheet for easy viewing and customization. Names of individuals that show up as a result of a query are automatically returned with a hotlink. With one click, the succession management team can access the resume and development plan.

The system also allows HR to download talent pipelines and metric reports. The output from the pipeline drives the succession plan, which is color coded and easy to read and understand. For higher positions, the system shows the employee who currently holds the position as well as three potential successors. Lilly can also call up summary metric reports that show real-time data on a number of prescribed measurement areas. The system provides tremendous functionality and usability. With the ability to use multiple search criteria, Lilly's succession management team can view any cut of the organization at a glance. The team makes sure its data is accurate, as invalid or inaccurate data is the fastest and easiest way to jeopardize or discredit the system. The team's goal in managing the Web site is for its decision makers to concentrate on outcomes, results, solutions, and placement, as opposed to questionable data or format.

The current intranet has already proven to be a positive experience. The internal feedback has been excellent, and Lilly reports a 50 percent increase in the number of individuals who have been loaded into the system during the first year of operation. The intranet site took three months to develop and was considerably cheaper than the system it replaced. A key discovery in using the intranet is the realization that multiple sublevel databases existed globally and rendered the corporate database incomplete and inaccurate, except at the highest levels. Every employee now has a global identification number that is synchronized with the system. With the succession management Web site in place, Lilly can operate from one central database.

## Identification Process

The process used at Lilly to identify high-potential employees happens in an annual, build-up process. It is moving away from twice annual review cycles in order to integrate them into one continuous, ongoing, and real-time process. Lilly uses three main categories which are described below, to classify all employees:

1. *Technical Leadership Potential*—demonstrates learning agility within his or her area of expertise and the ability to set strategic direction and lead thought in this area of expertise. Is this person recognized as a highly specialized expert in his or her technical discipline/function? Functions as an individual contributor or small group leader. Technical leadership candidates are not typically interested in or suited for functional or management positions.

2. *Functional Leadership Potential*—demonstrates learning agility within his or her function and area of expertise and highly developed skills in leading a functional organization. Usually the individual is recognized as much for functional expertise as managerial expertise. Functional leadership candidates are typically interested in and suited for managing one portion of the value chain.

3. *Cross-Functional Leadership Potential*—demonstrates significant learning agility across multiple functions and areas of expertise and highly developed skills in leading a multifunctional organization. Cross-functional leadership candidates are typically interested in and suited for managing across the value chain.

# Identification Tools

Every organization that has a firm grasp on managing succession has a trusted bag of tools it can open to make the job easier. Lilly is no exception. The following paragraphs highlight two of Lilly's most successful and useful tools—the talent identification questionnaire and the use of CEO reviews.

## Talent Identification Tool

The talent identification tool is used as early as possible after an employee is hired (and on the youngest talent) to create a diverse and voluminous candidate list for open positions. This tool assesses more than 18,000 associates all over the world. The six-page talent identification questionnaire was developed both by internal and external consultants (Lominger and Center for Creative Leadership) and targets three key factors:

1. *Performance*—track record of results; strong development or demonstration of management competencies

2. *Learning Agility*—willingness and ability to learn new skills under first time, tough, or different conditions

3. *Derailment Factors*—does not value working at higher levels, does not adhere to Lilly values, or exhibits other barriers to achieving potential

The data pulled from the talent identification tool guide the supervisor in determining an upward potential rating. The comparison of competencies to performance determines the height of an associate's potential and talent. The results are validated in line management reviews and are then input into the intranet and formed into metrics that are reviewed up through the CEO.

## CEO Reviews

A key element of the succession management process at Lilly is the involvement of the CEO. The CEO reviews each of nine functional business units at least once every three years, with some key functions reviewed annually. The head of each functional business unit, along with human resources and the CEO, meet for a full day to evaluate and select talent within the particular business unit. The business unit owner and corresponding human resources functional head own the review process, and the succession management team facilitates the process by designing tools and processes so that the review is conducted effectively. Although each business unit has different needs, the succession management team ensures that the content collected is of value to participants.

The succession management team prescribes similar reviews with human resources once a year in each of the nine functional business units mentioned above. These meetings are owned by the business unit head and attempt to fill 500 high-level positions. The group identifies and develops potential associates, analyzes a succession plan, and discerns gaps in the road to progression.

## Developmental Activities

After Lilly identifies talent through the methods described above, it looks to development as the next logical step. Lilly usually searches internally to fill open positions, so having its candidates ready to move up is vital. The subsections that follow outline mentoring, career planning, 360-degree feedback process, group development reviews, and action learning.

### Mentoring

Mentoring at Lilly occurs both formally and informally. Several different groups have developed a formal mentoring program, and these structured programs usually spring up around a specific functional area or geographic region. For example, the information technology and finance groups have developed separate, formalized mentoring programs. A few years ago, Lilly began an executive mentoring program with twenty-five high-potential individuals. The pilot program ran for eighteen months and was structured in the sense that Lilly provided an orientation and matched each candidate with a suitable mentor. Periodic and separate debriefing sessions were set up between the group of twenty-five mentors and groups of twenty-five candidates. In these debriefing sessions, discussions were held to report what worked well and what could be improved. A few relationships didn't work out because the mentor and candidate were in different geographic locations, however, many participants have continued the relationship long after the eighteen months had passed. The first effort was deemed a success and the company is planning a second program.

## Career Planning—Individual Development Plans

Both the resume and development plan stem from the performance management process at Lilly. The resume details positions held, positions of interest, reporting levels within the organization (status levels), current location, and mobility information. The development plan is evolving into both a short-term perspective to improve current responsibilities and a longer-term perspective to reach full potential.

## 360-Degree Feedback

Lilly uses COMPASS, which is a 360-degree feedback tool to assess leadership behaviors. The 360-degree process, in the past, was primarily used for development. Employees were encouraged to share the results of the 360-degree evaluation with their supervisors, but it wasn't mandatory. Now, COMPASS is required for all management employees and is an important part of performance management.

## Group Development Review

Lilly's largest executive development program is the group development review (GDR). Approximately 500 individuals with the highest potential are targeted for a ninety-minute conversation among supervisors. The meeting is facilitated by an external, third-party consultant, so that no biases prevail. To affirm the potential of candidates and specify development needs, feedback is taken from the current and past supervisor, as well as the supervisor's peers. They discuss the strengths and weaknesses of the candidate and produce a detailed report. The report is cowritten by a Lilly employee and the external consultant. The supervisor then shares the results with the candidate, and together with HR they put a development plan and career plan in place. The talent identification tool, coupled with the group development review, validates and confirms candidate potential and provides input to both the development plan and career plan. Every candidate with executive director potential must go through the review. Approximately 300 individuals have already gone through a group development review, and the status of many associates has been validated because of the review.

## Action Learning (Leadership V)

Lilly believes that 70 percent of learning takes place on the job, 20 percent comes about through relationships and informal men-

toring, and 10 percent occurs in a structured program. To this
end, Lilly embarked on an action learning pilot program in 2001
called "Leadership V." This program takes place every other year
and centers around eighteen high-potential leaders. Individuals
come from all functions and must have executive potential. The
final list is approved by the CEO.

The goal of the program is to have the eighteen individuals
learn by dealing with a real business issue. The structured program
covers a six-week time frame, and the CEO chooses the business
issue (e-business was a recent topic). Week one (boot camp) is
spent off-site where knowledge, topical, academic, and direc-
tional experts introduce and explain the topic so that all participants have a starting point and a basic understanding of the issue.
Week two is spent back on the job. During week three, the participants are split into teams of two and are instructed to conduct
150 interviews across the world, which are targeted at customers,
suppliers, best practice organizations, subject matter experts, and
thought leaders. Within each group, those interviewees with an
understanding or knowledge of Lilly were interviewed about how
to move forward with regard to the chosen business issue. The
participants then have three and a half days to debrief, make decisions, prepare a presentation to the CEO, and recommend a
course of action.

# Measurement

The succession management team at Lilly has created metrics
using employee data and leverages SAP and Oracle as a backbone. The recent creation of its Web-enabled database has
allowed it to quickly measure the results of the succession man-

agement processes. Lilly has two key succession management measurements—the overall quantity of talent in its pipeline, and the number of succession plans where there are two or more "ready now" candidates. Both metrics play an important part in answering the question "Do we have enough talent for both the near-term and the long-term?"

Talent pipeline metrics look closely at the ratio between incumbents at a level and individuals with potential to that same level. There are specific goal ratios for each level of management (e.g., 3:1 for the director level). Additionally, both groups are segmented to specifically track diversity. Lilly tracks the percent of incumbents and potentials at each level for gender, race/ethnicity (US only), geographic origin and certain experiences (e.g., cross-functional assignments). Lilly believes diversity is a critical element of business success in that if employees actually reflect the interests of customers, they are likely to make better decisions. They also purport that improvement of diversity of its "potentials" is a leading indicator of the diversity of its overall population. Querying the database allows Lilly to pinpoint these top successors and put development plans in place to reach its diversity and cross-functionality goals.

The succession plan metrics help the company understand the readiness of the pipeline and where gaps exist. Lilly understands how many "ready now" candidates it has for its top 500 positions. Similarly, it also understands where there are no "ready now" candidates and uses that information as a workflow trigger for executive recruiting activities. Additionally, analysis is done to understand how "thin" the pipeline might be. Metrics are gathered to determine how many individuals are on more than three succession plans as a "ready now" candidate.

The succession management team maintains additional metrics that the CEO presents to the board of directors. The team has created a funnel diagram that divides into potential managers, directors, executive directors, vice presidents, and senior vice presidents. At each level, the group can provide the number of incumbents and potential candidates identified. Those incumbents can be broken down into gender, race, experience outside home country, nationality, and cross-functional experience. The succession management team also puts together a quarterly scorecard that tracks progress on goals, tracks positional and pipeline data, and communicates the succession plan. This is reported to HR, which then shares the scorecard with the executive team. Currently, high-level metrics are in place; however, more specific measurement is forthcoming, which will include:

❏ Key positions filled and promoted through the succession plans

❏ Individuals that are currently ready for promotions for more than three positions

❏ Individuals who have potential at two levels higher than their current one

## Keys to Success and Future Goals

The succession management group's achievements have made significant advancements for Lilly. Two keys Lilly offers for success are to implement one consistent and simple process and one reliable technology solution.

At Lilly, the most important success factor is the intranet site. This is a universal and viable tool in the organization that has helped formulate metrics, manage knowledge, and continuously fill open positions. Again, much success is credited to the organization's culture of valuing professional development. The Lilly employees understand that passing up opportunities, hoarding information, and/or promoting the wrong people can destroy an organization.

Other keys to success include making the process mandatory, sufficient, and appropriate communication to the right people (the ones using the database), and piloting the program by rolling it out slowly to all employees. Future areas of opportunity include bridging SAP more seamlessly into succession management, moving to a stronger free-market approach to staffing, and winning the war for talent. Lilly also hopes to balance development learning and deep expertise learning while remaining externally focused. And like any organization, Lilly is trying to do all of this without introducing too much change too quickly.

## PanCanadian Petroleum
Industry: Petroleum
Headquarters: Calgary, Alberta, Canada
Revenues: $1 billion (2000)
Employees: 2,000 (2000)

The integration of two leading North American oil and gas explorers and producers, Alberta Energy Company Ltd. and PanCanadian Energy Corporation, on April 4, 2002, resulted in one of the world's largest independent petroleum companies, EnCana Corporation. The PanCanadian succession planning system has been merged into the new firm. The following case is based on the original research with APQC.

Headquartered in Calgary, Alberta, PanCanadian Petroleum Limited was a leading North American energy company active in the exploration, production, and marketing of natural gas, crude oil, and natural gas liquids. Core areas include the Western Basin, Canada's east coast, the Gulf of Mexico, and the United Kingdom. Founded in 1971, PanCanadian was named one of Canada's best companies to work for in 2000 and 2001 by the *Globe* and *Mail's Report on Business*. Key success factors include:

- ❑ Strong commodity prices
- ❑ Supply and demand fundamentals
- ❑ Operational excellence
- ❑ Disciplined strategy execution
- ❑ Innovative people
- ❑ Successful acquisitions
- ❑ Technological expertise
- ❑ Exploration

Aligned with the business strategy, succession management is action oriented through continuous dialogue, risk mitigation, and follow-up work. Rewarding leadership, initiative, and diversity of thought were instilled within PanCanadian's values and the company's efforts for continuous learning and a shared responsibility for developing skills. Because succession management was believed to be a strong predictor of success, PanCanadian used this system as a strategic business tool. And with the CEO as the champion of the process, succession management was a priority on PanCanadian's corporate agenda. By keeping the process simple and focused on people (rather than on the application), PanCanadian ensured that succession management directly aligned with the strategic business plan, the planning and budgeting cycle, and the people strategy.

Tailored to PanCanadian's unique needs, culture, and history, succession management was owned and supported by HR; line management owned the deliverables. The needs of the business drove the process; in turn, the process drove leadership, management, and other discipline development programs and investments.

To meet business requirements, PanCanadian defined succession management as an anticipative, aggressive, and flexible process that managed the demand and supply of key leadership talent through:

- ❑ Business and trend analysis

- ❑ Identification of current and emerging key positions

- ❑ Identification of high-potential and high-professional and technical employees

- ❑ Development of those employees

- ❑ Risk management

# Roles

Within human resources, the Centre of Excellence (COE) designed and integrated the program, facilitated it, and managed data for succession management. HR business partners consulted and supported succession management for general managers and their direct-report leadership teams. Professional and technical succession management was managed by a separate technology COE, consisting of active participation and decision making by operations and engineering managers. PanCanadian's CEO was the key driver and sponsor for succession management, and a sen-

ior management committee of vice presidents stewarded the process at the corporate level. At a business level, general managers
guided the process by completing succession management analyses, taking action to address issues, and participating in a people
conference. Key positions for succession management included
any direct reporting position to the president and senior vice presidents or any business management or professional and technical
leadership positions that must have planned successors. Key individuals were identified using six categories:

1. High-potential employees (category A)

2. High-potential employees (category B)

3. High-professional and technical employees (category A)

4. High-professional and technical employees (category B)

5. Bright-light employees

6. Critical skills employees

A high-potential employee had the potential to move up a
business management leadership path. Category A was considered
ready for promotion within the next couple of years, and Category
B within the next three to five years. A high-professional and technical employee had the potential to move up a professional and
technical leadership path and was also divided into either category A or B.

A "bright-light employee" exemplified leadership potential
and often required targeted investment to ensure retention. Employees placed in succession management talent pools were required to continually earn this designation. High-potential
employees were aware of their standing because managers paid
particular attention to their career management and develop-

ment. Although the larger work force was unaware of the succession management process, managers had ongoing conversations with high-potential and high-professional and technical employees to discuss development. Those not included in the talent pool were managed, motivated, and trained as valued contributors.

# Historical Context

The main driver for PanCanadian's internal program was PanCanadian's president and CEO, who assigned HR's Centre of Excellence to steward the process. Additionally, the CEO mandated attendance at a people conference, which is a forum to discuss current and future organizational requirements for leadership talent. For the first people conference, executive leaders spent three days identifying high-potential employees for business management leadership positions. Three hundred and sixty-degree feedback results were integrated, and succession plan management issues were identified. Within the context of continuous improvement, the information gathered for the people conference was expanded to include the identification of high-professional and technical employees and bright lights.

At the next people conference, risk management and mitigation were introduced, and improvements were made on data management and reporting. Key stakeholder input determined the size and scope of the succession management effort. Promotions, appointments, and development decisions were affected by this information. Conversations focused mainly on the talent pool, as well as development and action plans. The development of a succession plan was precipitated by anticipated leadership shortages (given competitive environments and demographics) and assessments of the leadership cadre. Within the context of the people strategy, leaders focused on the human resource needs of the organization and managed leadership excellence as a key component to the business.

## The People Strategy

In 1997, PanCanadian initiated a people strategy in conjunction with the current competitive strategy to achieve long-term business goals. The people strategy outlined the corporate approach to employee management and cultural requirements in support of the business plan. Developed and refreshed annually, the people strategy used the organization's business strategy as a base to understand cultural requirements, such as agility and innovation. The strategy identified components to attract and retain people, in part through development and succession management. Career planning, development, and management were separate from succession management but complemented the organizational continuity focus. Both succession management and career planning focused on employee development and alignment with corporate goals. Career planning was a systematic process of assessing an employee's attributes, such as skills and interests, whereas career development activities prepared individuals for meaningful work in the future. Career management enhanced the performance of employees by incorporating insights from individual career planning and career development activities.

## Risk Mitigation

The success of succession management was based on whether business objectives were met and limited talent-discontinuity risks occurred. Therefore, PanCanadian had a risk mitigation plan that managed talent discontinuity. The plan focused on high-risk positions with limited internal bench-strength, skills that were in short supply and previous mitigation efforts that had achieved limited success.

Mitigation strategies for high-risk positions and high-risk employees spanned the following spectrum:

❑ Hire externally to fill vacancies

❑ Borrow talent from other areas within or outside the company

❑ Exit of talent as needed

❑ Incent talent to provide rewards and compensate to encourage the attraction and retention of leadership talent

❑ Develop talent to ensure focused personal development plans are in place

## Leadership Competencies

Leadership competencies were evaluated biannually in preparation for the 360-feedback process. A combination of academic research, assessment of top performers, and future focus (strategic fit) was used to determine competencies needed for the future.

Leadership competencies were originally developed with the help of an external consultant. The following leadership competencies were viewed as being applicable to all management levels:

❑ Visionary qualities

❑ Effective communication

❑ Decisiveness and follow-through

❑ Business acumen

❑ People/team management

❑ Innovation

❑ Change management

Visionary leaders, it was believed, continually assess the external environment to identify trends, issues, and developing situations. They identify advantageous paths of action through a systemic assessment of business, social, environmental, and technological trends. By understanding the bigger picture, they anticipate and exploit key opportunities and potential challenges to create competitive advantage for the organization. A leader with effective communication recognizes the necessity of a meaningful context for planning and action. This leader gathers timely information in order to make sense of a situation, event, or context. Effective communication begins with strong interpersonal skills and with the personal qualities of honesty, integrity, and candor. By being consistent in words and deeds, this leader establishes increasing levels of trust and cooperation.

A decisive leader takes appropriate action when necessary to execute and implement plans and projects. This leader commits resources in a timely, principled, balanced, and effective manner and minimizes the effects of unforeseen consequences. This leader knows when to take action independently and when the action of others is required. Taking action is based on self-confidence, a strong desire to achieve, and the ability to assume authority.

Leaders with business acumen understand how organizations develop and execute strategies. Such a leader creates effective work processes that add value to the organization, constructs sound business cases for projects, develops execution plans with full knowledge of the intended benefits and risks, and also creates effective reporting structures to ensure success. A leader demonstrating this competency identifies and uses sound business metrics and demonstrates solid value to the organization through clear and accurate performance measures. A leader demonstrating team management works effectively with and through others to produce organizational success. This leader recognizes, solicits, and respects the diverse contributions made by others to increase involvement and buy-in and to ensure effective problem solving and efficient action.

An innovative leader captures attention and attracts resources for new ideas. Such a leader recognizes that learning and creativity are essential to the creation of new knowledge and creates an atmosphere that encourages learning. This leader also understands that the knowledge generated from learning needs to be managed and utilized effectively to be of value to the organization. Because innovation is often a collaborative activity, this leader supports group learning and personally encourages communities of practice. Also, this leader recognizes that the value of knowledge is not only in its content but also in the renewal rate.

A leader demonstrating change management is capable of developing and initiating change processes. Such a leader identifies, utilizes, and combines the necessary resources (people, processes, and technology) to create effective processes. Resilience, resourcefulness, and adaptability are necessary to withstand change, and this leader develops and communicates clear reasons for change and creates effective plans for their implementation. This leader ensures alignment of focus and effort through efficient use of resources and adapts as required.

# Making Decisions for Technical Leadership

Stewarded by the technology COE, professional and technical leadership at PanCanadian included engineers, geologists, geophysicists, chiefs, and advisers. Meetings with operational and engineering managers were held throughout the year and used the succession management framework to decide:

❑ Staff planning

❑ Compensation (base pay and variable bonus)

❑ Promotions

❑ Employee development

This information was shared at the annual people conference.

# Decision-Making Matrix

Developed in 1999 and modified in 2000, the decision-making matrix was used by technical and business leaders to make decisions on high-potential, high-professional, and technical leadership talent. It also incorporated actions for individual development. For example, if an employee was considered high performing with little potential for upward advancement in the organization, the action required was to continue developing his or her skills in the current position. An employee's performance was based on an ongoing demonstration of values and competencies and achievement of results. Potential was based on the ability to move up the organization structure. Although PanCanadian did not explicitly distinguish promotable employees from high-potential employees, high-potential employees were seen as being able to handle responsibility at two or more levels above their current assignment.

# Developmental Activities

The CEO and executive team profiled protégés at the people conference and increased development by assigning projects to high-potential employees. All high-potential and high-professional and technical employees had development plans in place, and all employees were encouraged to have development plans as part of their performance management.

PanCanadian utilized the following development activities as a framework for development:

- ❑ Internal, informal mentoring

- ❑ Formal and informal coaching

- ❑ Job rotation

- ❑ Placement with specific bosses

- ❑ 360-degree feedback

The 360-degree feedback program was used to support ongoing development of leaders in relation to specific leadership skills and PanCanadian's culture. PanCanadian began using 360-degree feedback as part of performance assessment in 2000. The program was developed with external consulting support. Based on the leadership competencies outlined earlier, the results were shared with the employee and his or her supervisor, who was accountable for feedback, analysis, and development plans. The program was mandatory, and the scope included first-line supervisors and above (i.e., anyone with more than three direct reports). Every June, the results were received and provided the opportunity for aggregating survey results.

## Management Development

The Centre of Excellence owned management development. Some examples of internal and external courses are:

- ❑ Management forum (PanCanadian's internal MBA program)
- ❑ Executive development programs
- ❑ Executive MBA
- ❑ Online learning
- ❑ Conferences

The management forum was a two-year management development initiative that enabled leaders to adapt quickly and efficiently in a dynamic business environment. The forum was focused on developing three core competencies:

1. Managing performance
2. Change and innovation within the context of self-management, management of teams, and relationships
3. Knowledge management

The purpose of the forum was to provide sound management education by bringing contemporary best practices to participants. The management forum was specifically created to align management competencies with strategic direction to meet current and future needs. The leadership community used the forum to share existing knowledge and new findings.

Components of the forum included:

❑ Performance contracting

❑ Self-assessments

❑ Coaching sessions

❑ Learning modules

❑ Team assignment

❑ Integration of PanCanadian programs

Programs that were integrated into the forum included people strategy, total compensation, diversity, wellness, 360-degree feedback, change management framework, knowledge management, and performance management. These tools fit into the overall development program at integral points in the succession management cycle.

# Keeping Succession Management Dynamic

With an emphasis at executive meetings, succession management information was updated at least quarterly. Monthly reporting of development opportunities and key talent allowed for movement and special assignment of employees. Employee career preference clearly influenced the developmental process. Ongoing integration and alignment with other human resources programs (e.g., accountability agreements and 360-degree feedback) ensured that succession management remained dynamic.

## Ensuring Diversity

Diversity awareness was generated to ensure that bias did not negatively influence decisions made. While no specific diversity targets were set, in-session facilitation eliminated bias in decision making.

Mental and occupational categories were inherent in discussions of high-potentials and high-professional and technical talent; postanalysis included gender and age considerations. A diversity framework was used to guide preliminary discussions that integrated diversity in the succession management process.

## Movement

The succession management program facilitated the movement of people across organizational units to broaden development and skills and to meet business needs. However, other systemic considerations may have indirectly restricted movement (e.g., the risk of jeopardized production targets).

## Measures

In 2000, an external consultant assessed the process and identified areas of improvement to incrementally mature the process. Succession management was continually assessed, along with

other human resources programs. PanCanadian had no specifically measurable results indicating the effectiveness of the succession management process and relied primarily on anecdotal
feedback. Typically, the emphasis was to move to richer dialogue
to incorporate risk mitigation and emphasize action-orientation,
as well as to shorten the cycle time for data management. The
result measures were identified and tracked, with the focus including (but not limited to) the number of high-potential employees
who terminated their employment, readiness of the employees,
and length of time key positions remained vacant. PanCanadian
generated basic succession management reports such as individual
profiles, high-potential and high-professional/technical employees talent pools, key positions and bench-strength, and analyses
of position and people data by gender, generation, level, and risk

Succession management was monitored throughout the year
via quarterly updates, report generation and analysis, leadership
board meetings, and feedback from human resources business
partners. Employee development plans were updated annually. It
was the responsibility of the supervising manager and the employee to ensure that they were realized. Copies were included
and distributed as part of the succession management information.

## Success Factors

Key elements to successful succession management seemed to include having a focused, systemic process linked to real-time business drivers and active participation of senior executives. With
clear measures of success and clear standardized criteria for high-
potential and high professional and technical nominations, suc-

cession management attempted to achieve standardized application throughout the organization.

## Lessons Learned

Human resources professionals at PanCanadian believed that they had learned the importance of spending less time on who the high-potentials and high professional and technical people were and more time on thinking about how to leverage, foster, and retain them. They also felt that creating a sense of urgency was always a challenge in succession management, and that integration with other human resource management and business processes was critical to sustainability. As they reflected on the challenges at the time of the merger, their unaccomplished objectives included:

❑ Moving business management leadership succession management to the business unit and general manager level

❑ Further integrating and aligning succession management with strategic planning and operations management business decisions

❑ Further integration and alignment with other human resource management programs

❑ Leveraging the risk management strategies to a greater degree

❑ Further identifying high-risk areas (current and emerging, people and positions)

❑ Incorporating growth assignments for high-potential and high-professional and technical talent

❑ Establishing clear measures to track progress

❑ Strengthening the overall process based on key stakeholder feedback

❑ Improving front-end reporting facility of the ACCESS database and making it available to the business with the appropriate security measures

## Sonoco Products Company
Industry: Manufacturing
Headquarters: Hartsville, S.C.
Revenues: $2.8 billion (estimated 2003)
Employees: 18,000 (2003)
Web Page: www.sonoco.com

A diverse, global corporation with multiple divisions, Sonoco Products Company is one of the world's largest makers of industrial and consumer packaging products. Products include flexible packaging, composite cans, tubes, cores, cones, and wire and cable reels. For the consumer markets, the company produces packaging for food processors, food stores, and makers of household products. Sonoco operates in thirty-two countries, with approximately 300 plants. Having recently celebrated its 100-year anniversary, Sonoco recognizes that many things have changed in its industry over the past century. The industry is more competitive than ever before, and with fewer resources and more demands on people's time, it is more important than ever that the company have a system in place to identify and engage future leaders.

# Deploying a Succession Management Program

When the current vice president of human resources arrived at Sonoco, the company had been engaged in what it called "succession planning." However, a review of the files and records revealed that although some good things had been conducted in this area, these activities appeared to have been undertaken as one-time efforts performed to some degree in isolation. Additionally, no follow-up, such as action plans, had been performed during the process. Today, one of the key success factors in Sonoco's succession management process is that the system forms a basis for making decisions and taking action.

To date, Sonoco's efforts in succession planning focus on the company's top 300 to 400 employees, the top management group. And for the board of directors, that group is focused even further to the top twenty or so managers. Efforts with the remaining exempt employee population have mirrored the overall corporate efforts to manage succession. However, with the recent restructuring Sonoco experienced, corporate HR focuses on division-level efforts in succession planning.

From an executive perspective, the corporate HR group at Sonoco believes that there are six key steps a company should take to create a succession planning system:

1. Secure the time and involvement of the senior management group.

2. Obtain input from the employees or managers that are the focus of the succession planning system.

3. Obtain input from several levels of management.

4. Use the data from the succession planning process to make decisions.

5. Link the succession planning process to corporate strategy.

6. Link succession planning to organizational development commitments.

First, the HR group (or whichever group is in charge of succession planning) needs the time and commitment of the company's senior management. Sonoco's eight-member executive committee (including the CEO, vice president of HR, CFO, and top group vice presidents who have multiple divisions working for them) spends a full week every year focused on formal discussions concerning succession planning.

The second major challenge is obtaining input from the employees or managers who are part of the top 300 to 400 employees focused on by the process. Acquiring that employee input is critical. HR obtains input from the individual via the process and provides the individual with information on how upper management views that person. It is a good opportunity to let key people know where they stand, their promotability, and more.

Third, obtaining input from several levels of management is also essential. A direct supervisor may indicate that a person is "outstanding" and can perform a certain job. However, someone else may identify another aspect or skill area that the person needs to be promoted. Multiple viewpoints provide a better perspective on an individual and are a healthy part of the succession planning process.

Fourth, using data from the succession planning process to make decisions must become standard procedure. At the end of the weeklong formal process with the executive committee, HR summarizes the gathered data from the various divisions. When there are job openings, senior management revisits the summary of information generated from the succession planning process.

According to the vice president of HR, Sonoco's CEO likes the succession planning process so well that he automatically comes to her when a position opens to discuss likely candidates for the job.

Because Sonoco has been performing succession planning for several years, the process has almost become automatic. Using the data in this manner lends credibility to the process for the managers; what they say to people is in fact what they are doing. It also provides a reality check by indicating where there might be holes or weak areas in the candidate pool.

Fifth, a company's succession planning system needs to be linked to the corporate strategy. It should focus on the positions and people critical to the success of the company. The people involved in succession planning should look at three things: (1) the strategy of the company and future direction, (2) what critical jobs make the difference, and (3) what is being done to develop those positions.

Finally, succession planning needs to be linked to the company's development commitments. Where are development dollars being spent? Where are development efforts being focused? Development money and efforts should focus on those people identified as promotable. Sonoco also uses succession planning to assist in making compensation decisions. There should be a clear link between succession planning and reward dollars.

## Succession Planning Process

One problem Sonoco encountered early in its succession planning process was a lack of guidelines to help managers prepare for the process. Each division wanted to do things its own way, and this made the review process difficult because the materials looked different for every division. To address this issue, corporate HR set the schedule for the review four to six months in advance, which allowed the members of the executive committee plenty of time to reserve time on their calendars.

Corporate HR then sent a notice to the various divisions asking them to schedule succession planning on their own calendars in accordance with the executive committee's calendar. Each division was given a time frame (e.g., one to two hours) for their presentation to the committee, based on the size of the division and on corporate HR's estimate of how much time it would take the division senior management teams to go through the reviews. Additionally, corporate HR provided the divisions with instructions on preparing the materials for the presentation, which they were asked to follow exactly. In this way, corporate HR tried to ensure that the materials were as consistent as possible.

The divisions were asked to include seven items in their presentations:

1. A demographic breakdown of the salaried exempt work force for the U.S. division

2. An organization chart showing the division general manager (GM) or corporate staff head and his or her direct reports

3. A succession plan chart with candidates for the positions, including the division general manager

4. A performance/promotability matrix that ranks all of the individuals listed on the organization chart above and a

second matrix that ranks all of the succession candidates from the succession chart

5. Career and development profiles for each person listed in the organization and succession charts

6. Employee satisfaction scores using the employee satisfaction survey index

7. Key issues in the division or corporate department and how they are being addressed

The demographic data, using PeopleSoft software, includes age, years of service, education level attained, and race and gender. Only divisions within the United States are asked to provide a demographic breakdown of their salaried exempt work force, since there are currently no blended systems outside the United States. Corporate HR and the executive committee found the demographic data interesting but were not sure what to do with it. The divisions will probably not be required to provide this on a regular basis. The divisions used HRCharter software to create the organization chart and the succession chart. To plot the successors for each group, they employed ExecuTRACK software. A tool called the "performance and promotability matrix" was used to rank all the individuals listed on both charts. Sonoco began utilizing this tool approximately five years ago. The matrix contains three levels of performance and three levels of promotability. Each division reviewed all of the people to be included in their succession planning process and plotted them somewhere on the matrix. Six cuts of the matrix were reviewed. The top two layers were the direct reports to the division GMs and the next level down of direct reports (i.e., successor candidates). Each was plotted on separate matrices. The remaining four cuts included a

matrix on regional manufacturing managers, regional sales managers, sales people below the manager level, and plant or location
managers. Corporate HR asked that each division produce these
six matrices and bring them with the other review materials. The
divisions pulled information for the career and development profiles for each person listed in the organization and succession
planning charts from the individual's performance management
document. Performance management documents were built using
Lotus Notes, which is part of the integrated software used by Sonoco. (The PeopleSoft employee database is located there as
well.) Additionally, each division was asked to use the employee
satisfaction survey index to provide a rank order listing from high
to low of all of the plants in the division based on the percentage
of favorability. Survey index history goes back to 1997, and the
divisions included the latest data for all plants back to that date.

Sonoco mandates that these satisfaction surveys be conducted
for every operation, at minimum, once every three years. Some
do it more frequently. Corporate HR calls this an organization
review instead of succession planning, but it was included as part
of the overall review process.

Corporate HR also asked all divisions to provide a listing of
key issues within their organization and how those issues were
being addressed. HR also requested information concerning division or corporate department use of performance management,
360-degree feedback reviews, and the status of training and development efforts. Corporate HR asked all divisions to consistently
complete reports and books. In fact, HR sent the divisions a template to use. Most divisions indicated that this was very helpful in
providing them with needed guidance. Corporate HR and the
executive committee found that having a consistent process
across the entire corporation made it easier to perform the analysis and provide functional, actionable data back to the divisions.

Ideally, Sonoco would like to perform the succession planning review every year; in reality, it occurs approximately every eighteen months.

Each division is asked to identify only those candidates within its business units, for two reasons. First, a division will occasionally identify successors from other divisions, thereby feeling that it does not have to worry about developing its own people. Secondly, it prevents one person from being identified as the successor for an inordinate number of jobs. It is permissible for a division to indicate that it has no successor for a position, but the executive committee will question the division's senior management team about this lack. This absence of qualified successors is not tolerated two years in a row. The actual executive committee review process is easier to administer if candidate identification is kept on a divisionalized basis. An objective of corporate HR and the executive committee is to do a better job of moving people across divisions.

# The Performance Management System

Sonoco's performance management system requires that performance management documents be completed by the end of the first quarter of each year. A division prepares the succession planning components for its organization in the first quarter. Employees are asked to update and complete their performance management documents in that first quarter as well.

Sonoco's performance management system is built around eight competencies: four core and four leadership competencies. Each competency is built around certain behaviors.

# Core Competencies

1. Business and technical knowledge

2. Communication

3. Customer satisfaction through excellence (internal and external customers)

4. Teamwork and collaboration

# Leadership Competencies

1. Leadership and commitment

2. Coaching and developing

3. Innovation

4. Diversity

Defining core competencies at Sonoco is a way of communicating performance expectations to employees. The competencies were initially developed with the assistance of Developmental Dimensions International (DDI). Corporate HR defined the four core competencies for the total company (i.e., exempt and nonexempt employees). At the time Sonoco developed the core competences for the company, several similar divisional pilots were going on independently. A team of GMs was assembled to look into this issue. The mission was to define a new leadership development process for Sonoco.

A performance management process had already been initiated, and the team felt that it ought to be based on the core competencies. Concurrently, the HR Council approved a standardized performance management system across the entire corporation with common core competencies. The HR Council and line executive team agreed on the same set of competencies.

The next step was to define behaviors for those competencies. Materials from DDI were used for this activity. Additionally, a group of approximately thirty senior managers in the company were interviewed about their success factors.

An HR team presented the recommended competencies (with behaviors) to a group of approximately forty-five senior managers and asked them to challenge this competency set. After these refined competencies were put in place, the top 300 employees were asked to participate in a 360-degree feedback exercise based on the new competencies. At the time of the best practice visit, Sonoco had more requests for 360-degree feedback then it could manage.

After the first 360-degree feedback exercise, it became clear that there wasn't enough guidance for the employees to act on the feedback received. The following year, specific training was offered on creating and implementing a development plan. Training was done with division HR managers, so that they could work with divisional employees. There is now a regular review and assessment to improve the 360-degree feedback process within Sonoco.

## Identifying the Talent Pool

At the division level, key outcomes from the succession planning process include:

❏ Identification of successors for key positions within the company (specifically, the general managers and their direct reports)

❏ An assessment of group strength (e.g., is the company weak in bench strength for certain areas (such as plant managers)

❏ Identification of key people issues

The talent pool is created by data collected from plant, area, and general managers. In their meetings to identify high potentials for the talent pool, the following principles are emphasized:

❏ *Build from the bottom up*—Succession planning starts at the bottom of the talent pool with the plant managers and moves up through the area managers to GMs.

❏ *Involve those who are closest*—In the assessment meetings, the people who are closest to the individuals being evaluated should be given primary consideration. Often it is the individual's direct supervisor who is the principal voice.

❏ *Use the performance data*—The performance management documents of those being evaluated should always be available in these meetings. Other data should be looked at as well, including employee profiles (including education and work history) and additional interactions and observations of the management team regarding the individual being reviewed.

❏ *Use consensus decision making*—To insure fairness and objectivity, the decision making should involve more than just the supervisor.

❑ *Start early*—Many discussions will take place, so assessment
is not necessarily a sequential process. While many inputs
come together in the first quarter of a year, succession
planning should be a focus of managers throughout the
year.

# Group Level Meetings

At the division level, the vice president, area managers, and the
division's HR manager meet off-site for a full day. This group uses
the consensus process to determine where each of the forty plant
managers falls on the performance or promotability matrix. Other
people may be invited to attend to gain a comprehensive picture
of the person being evaluated. For example, the sales and marketing divisions are very closely linked, so representatives from both
organizations attend each other's meetings. The key is to involve
managers who observe the people being evaluated on a daily basis.
The group looks at the performance management document of
each manager as that person is discussed. The group reviews his or
her competencies, completed objectives for the year, and personal
development plans. The prior year's succession planning data is
also brought to the meeting to determine if the individual has
moved on the performance matrix.

At the plant manager level, the purpose of the meeting is to
identify performance or promotability factors, rather than successors. The outcome of this meeting is a pool of potential successors
rather than a few individuals identified as a potential successor
for a particular plant. The outcome of these discussions is an understanding of total group strength. Everyone at the plant manager level is plotted on the matrix, and divisional strengths and
weaknesses are discussed. The group also formulates plans for em-

ployee development. Special attention is directed to those individuals in the high-potential and low-potential boxes of the performance and promotability matrix. The group can then take action based on the results of plotting everyone on the matrix.

A challenge faced by Sonoco is what to do when you have more people identified as exceptional performers than you have positions in which to move them. This can be a critical issue. The company puts together action plans around that issue that included such possibilities as moving individuals to another division, giving travel assignments, or merely continuing to focus on their compensation and development.

The matrix itself is not shared with individuals; however, area managers do discuss general information about where the individual is on the matrix (e.g., whether this person is viewed as promotable).

## Area Manager Meetings

This example focuses on the successors to the division's vice president, generally the area managers who have responsibility for multiple plants. Besides that division's area managers, other people outside that organization are also evaluated. (e.g., people from the sales, finance, or technology divisions or corporate areas). Therefore, discussions held during this meeting often include other people who might not be in the traditional career path for area management. These meetings are smaller and more focused. The people involved include the vice president of manufacturing, the GM of that organization, and an HR representative. This in-depth discussion looks at the same data as other succession planning groups: performance management information, succession

planning data from prior years, and other observations the supervisors may have from discussions with people who work with the
potential successors. The team discusses the person's strengths,
capabilities, and opportunities for development. However, the
outcomes of this meeting are that successors are identified, a development plan for each individual is in place, and each successor
is plotted on the matrix.

# General Manager Meetings

Even fewer people are involved in the meeting to discuss the general manager's successors. The GM plays a large role in proposing
whom he or she sees as a successor. The executive committee
reviews the GM's suggested successor(s), but the GM is the key
person in this process. Another focus of discussion with the GM
of each division is to review all the prior work, all the matrices,
from earlier discussions regarding plant and area managers. The
executive committee and GMs review this data in detail and extract information from it.

Questions are asked such as, "What is this telling us?" and,
"What kind of needs do we have?" The group discusses the strategy of each business and what it is trying to accomplish through
it. The group uses this exercise to identify key issues that surface
as it reviews the data. These discussions often reveal much of the
value of succession planning. For example, during the process the
group may realize that there is a lack of leadership depth to meet
potential growth in Mexico. Another example is realizing that
there is a large number of exceptional managers but few positions
open for them.

These discussions and other activities culminate in presentations to the executive committee, usually in the July–August time frame. Afterward, follow-through is required to communicate to the divisions about the results of these sessions. The divisions are reminded to focus on individuals in the high and low potential boxes of the matrix, to look at the key issues, and to act on them. Key issues then become part of an individual's performance management plan, either as an objective or as a development area. Every staff group undergoes the same process.

# Executive Committee Review Process

The executive committee review process takes place in the board-room at Sonoco headquarters in Hartsville, South Carolina. The divisions' vice president GM attends with his or her senior HR person. Occasionally, the GM may bring a senior manufacturing person as well or perhaps someone from another division. Each meeting starts with a review of that division's organization and successor charts. Discussion then moves to the matrix and the placement of people within it. The executive committee questions the decisions made by the senior management team, asking such questions as, "What makes this person promotable?" and, "What are the plans for this individual?" These meetings are conducted as an open forum, and executives may pose any questions they like. The goal is to try to create consensus on the placement of key individuals. Follow-up meetings are set with the HR managers from each of the operating units.

Presentation materials from the executive committee meeting are available for review. Additionally, corporate HR also discusses the development plans for the appropriate individuals with the divisional HR managers. The divisional managers are reminded that each manager should review his or her last 360-degree feedback data to ensure that areas that need additional attention are adequately addressed. The divisions are charged with responsibility for following up to ensure that developmental plans are in place and being worked on with input from the individual's supervisor. Plans are generally established for a later session to revisit the development plans and progress that was made.

# Talent Pools

Business divisions are asked to identify potential candidates for jobs because this information is needed for base data input. However, corporate HR does not identify candidates for a job in terms of the analysis it performs. Instead, HR develops candidate pools. For example, for any of the vice president general managers, corporate HR looks across the organization for those individuals who have been identified as potential successors for a vice president general manager opening. A cross-corporation pool is created that includes individuals who should be considered. Therefore, if one of these positions becomes available, the successor is pulled from this predetermined pool. There is also a pool for staff vice presidents.

The executive committee reviews and approves the names for each pool. If the committee has a problem with one of the names, this concern is explored. Sonoco wants to be able to choose people from the designated pool. If this is not possible, the system is not working well. The corporate target is for 80 to 90 percent of key appointments to be made from these pools. Disconnects may occur when the position is open now, but the people identified to be successors will not be ready for two to three years, or when the job has been modified so that some specialty might be required that the successors do not have.

Corporate HR also examines the number of individuals in each pool who are in the high-potential block on the performance and promotability matrix. A corporate-wide listing of all the people listed in this block is assembled for review.

Sonoco has operated with eight distinct talent pools:

1. Country managers (outside the United States)

2. Vice president, director level, for sales and marketing

3. Manager level, for sales and marketing

4. Vice president, director level, for manufacturing

5. Finance/IT positions

6. Human resources

7. Technology and engineering

8. Purchasing and other staff pools

These broad pools are reviewed for incumbents and all potential successors for the incumbents. This action is performed at the corporate and functional levels. Corporate HR takes this information back to the executive committee for an overview and one last reality check. Typically, few changes are made to the matrix at this point. These pools provide HR and the executive committee with a high-level view of the whole organization.

Corporate HR also looks at how many years a person has been on the succession planning list and what has happened to him or her over time. If a person keeps showing up on the list but has not moved (laterally) or been promoted, perhaps he or she should be taken off the list.

# Software Applications for Succession Management

A few years ago, Sonoco recognized the need to review its HR software applications. This review revealed a need for a new Human Resource Information System (HRIS) in order to maintain data on its employees. The firm selected PeopleSoft, a software system with HR and financial applications. This review also revealed that various tools were employed throughout the organization with pieces of information that would be helpful if they could all be brought into one package. There was also a desire to move from being paper based to using Web-based applications. A team was formed to review various applications and to identify ways to pull those distant pieces of information together. Social Security numbers were used to link U.S. programs together. For those divisions located outside the United States, identification numbers were created for all employees. Using these numbers, four programs were linked together to create a complete succession planning package (PeopleSoft, HRCharter, Lotus Notes, and ExecuTRACK).

The performance management system was already in place and utilized Lotus Notes. Every employee with access to Lotus Notes participated in the system. Only managers with a "need to know" can access an employee's record. The performance management document has four sections for each employee:

1. Objectives

2. Core and leadership competencies

3. Career and development plans

4. Comments

Information from the career and development plan section is extracted and linked back to the succession planning system. Additionally, the data in PeopleSoft is linked back to performance management documents.

Another challenge was to link succession planning to personal development needs and plans. This information existed in the performance management system, but linking it to the records of the individual in PeopleSoft to develop a true succession planning system was difficult. A team was assembled to review options that would allow this linkage. Sonoco was already utilizing the DOS version of ExecuTRACK; however, it was cumbersome and difficult to use, so the firm moved to the Clientserver version of ExecuTRACK. Now it is possible to extract information from the base data in PeopleSoft, putting it into the ExecuTRACK system and pulling information from the performance management system.

Personal information, reporting relationships, department division names, work history (internal and external), education, and educational history are now pulled from PeopleSoft. Other data including strengths, weaknesses, and areas of improvement can be extracted from the performance management system. Of course, systems are only as good as the information they possess. Each division has an administrator responsible for putting information in PeopleSoft and ensuring that information moved from PeopleSoft to ExecuTRACK is current and accurate. The ExecuTRACK system updates itself every night with any information added during the day. ExecuTRACK has enabled HR to move away from paper to a large degree and lessened the amount of time spent on the process as well. In about 1998, Sonoco began using the performance and promotability matrix to rank all the individuals listed on both the organization and successor charts. The performance and promotability matrix now pulls information back from ExecuTRACK.

The system uses the individual's readiness codes and places them on the chart. Names are listed in alphabetical order in each block. Criteria for determining performance level and promotability have been established. Once all of this information was pulled together, a need to produce charts for inclusion in the packets for the executive committee became apparent. An application called HRCharter was installed inside ExecuTRACK, so that someone working inside ExecuTRACK could generate a chart without having to exit the application. HRCharter merely requires a user to provide the name of the individual and to select the needed information (e.g., direct reports to the individual). The program pulls all the information together and places the data in a chart for the user. As information is updated, the charts can be updated as well by clicking on the update field.

Sonoco uses special assignments, task force assignments, and Six Sigma for development purposes. Assignments such as these are good for moving people out of their comfort zones and providing them with exposure to senior managers and other aspects of the business as well. They also provide a good opportunity for persons to demonstrate their capabilities.

## Monitoring and Assessing the Program

Sonoco does not perform any statistical analysis on its succession planning process. The firm believes that the best measure of the system is the degree of use and the number of candidates who can be successfully chosen from the succession planning process.

Divisions report that the new system has generated a 75 percent savings in time from previous years. The division administrators expect that the time will decrease further as they become more familiar with the system and address some of the issues, such as remote accessibility. There is a pull for the succession planning process from the divisions. The feedback has indicated that senior management enjoys the offsite meetings and supports the process.

Most of the information in this case study reflects what the divisions do to meet corporate requests. However, within the divisions the process is often pushed even further. Senior management teams here may use the process to review their shift supervisors. These teams find the succession planning process extremely valuable and believe that it helps them make good decisions. The performance and promotability matrix is 80 to 90 percent accurate in its predictions.

# Summary

An assessment of Sonoco's approach to succession management has convinced management that as there is more honesty in the system and as people get better at using it. There is greater fairness and consistency than before the system was refined and employed throughout the organization. Sonoco did go through a learning curve with its new system and recognizes several continuing challenges. Keeping tabs on the key people located away from corporate headquarters and outside the United States is difficult.

Another challenge is depth of leadership and preparing enough people for promotions without destroying the motivation of those who do not receive the promotions they seek. A third challenge is that most Sonoco promotions tend to come from within a functional area. One of their goals is to have more promotions from across divisions and functions. Remote access to the system provides another challenge to the company. For divisions outside Hartsville, accessing files and transfer time takes too long.

The final challenge to Sonoco's succession planning system is the need to revisit individual development plans and progress made on a timely basis. Although some divisions do this well, it is not done consistently across all divisions.

## Successful Succession Planning

According to the HR team at Sonoco, the following elements go into the making of a successful succession planning system:

- ❑ Senior management wants the process and uses it, which makes it more than just an exercise.

- ❑ It's practical to use.

- ❑ It's simple to use.

- ❑ It's built to solve the organization's particular succession planning needs.

- ❑ There is a commitment to applying it afterward.

# Research Methodology

Developed in 1993, the APQC consortium benchmarking methodology serves as one of the premier methods in the world for successful benchmarking. It is an extremely powerful tool for identifying best and innovative practices and for facilitating the actual transfer of those practices. The methodology is described below and illustrated in Figure App. B-1.

## Phase 1: Plan

Most of the study team had been involved in previous studies of leadership development in global firms, so they brought with

**CONSORTIUM BENCHMARKING MODEL**

Figure App. B-1. APQC four-phase methodology.

them a sense of firms that might be viewed as leaders in the
arena of succession management and planning. The study team,
using secondary research and other sources of information, identified a number of organizations that were believed to have
achieved a high degree of success in succession management.
Each identified organization was invited to participate in a
screening process. Based on the results of the screening process,
as well as company capacity or willingness to participate in the
study, the final list of potential partners was developed. Sponsors were also given a chance to finalize the list of firms to be
benchmarked.

A kickoff meeting was conducted during which the sponsors
solidified the study scope and gave input on the data collection
tools. Finalizing the data collection tools and piloting them
within the sponsor group concluded the planning phase.

# Phase 2: Collect

Two principal tools were used to collect information:

1. *Detailed Questionnaires:* quantitative questions were designed to collect objective, quantitative data across all participating organizations

2. *Site-Visit Guide:* qualitative questions that paralleled the focus areas in the detailed questionnaire; served to structure the discussion at site visits

All partners and sponsors completed the detailed questionnaire, and all five partner organizations hosted half-day site visits attended by sponsors, partners, and members of the study team. The APQC study team prepared written reports for each site visit and submitted them to the partner organizations for approval and/or clarification. These site visit reports were then distributed to all sponsor organizations with the final report at the conclusion of the study.

# Phase 3: Analyze

The subject matter experts and APQC analyzed both the quantitative and qualitative information gained from the data collection tools. The analysis examined the challenges organizations face in their succession management programs. The analysis of the data, as well as case examples taken from the site visits, is contained in the present book. While study sponsors had exclusive access to the data for one year after the completion of the research, the authors of this book contacted all of the benchmark firms to determine what changes had been made since the original data was collected. While the material reported herein has been updated, world-class succession systems are a moving target and are always under revision. Consequently, this book should be viewed as a snapshot rather than the current reality of any system.

# Phase 4: Adapt

Key lessons identified in the consortium study have, it is hoped, been adapted for improvements at sponsor organizations. APQC staff members have been available to help sponsors create action plans appropriate for the organization based on the results of this study. Readers are also expected to participate in this process. No firm should adopt all of the methods or system components described in the manuscript without tailoring them to fit their own special circumstances. These should, however, serve as a guide for what can be and is being done by some firms to respond to their particular and unique challenges.

# Index

# About the Authors

**Robert M. Fulmer** serves as Academic Director for Duke Corporate Education and is currently a Distinguished Visiting Professor at Pepperdine University.

A world expert in leadership, Bob has designed and delivered leadership development initiatives in twenty-two countries and on six continents. His research and writing have focused on future challenges of management, implementation of strategy, and leadership development as a lever for change efforts.

Bob's writings have been widely read in both academic and professional circles. He is the author of four editions of *The New Management* and coauthor of four editions of *A Practical Introduction to Business* as well as of *Crafting Competitiveness, Executive Development and Organizational Learning for Global Business, Leadership by Design,* and *The Leadership Investment.*

Bob received his first endowed chair at Trinity University and has served as director of corporate management development for Allied Signal, Inc., with worldwide responsibility for management development, ranging from first-line supervision to senior executives. He has also served as president of two management consulting firms specializing in human resource issues.

He was previously the W. Brooks George Professor of Management at the College of William and Mary and a visiting scholar at the Center for Organizational Learning at MIT. He also taught

Organization and Management at Columbia University's Graduate Business School. For six years, Bob was director of executive education at Emory University, where he directed the Executive MBA program as well as public and customized programs for general and functional managers.

Bob earned his MBA from the University of Florida and his Ph.D. from the University of California at Los Angeles.

**Jay A. Conger** is Professor of Organizational Behavior at the London Business School and Senior Research Scientist at the Center for Effective Organizations at the University of Southern California in Los Angeles. Formerly the executive director of the Leadership Institute at the University of Southern California, Jay Conger is one of the world's experts on leadership. You'll see him quoted in the *Wall Street Journal* analyzing people and trends in the executive suite and in the boardroom. In recognition of his extensive work with companies, *Business Week* named him 'number five' on its list of the world's top ten management gurus. The *Financial Times* described him as one of the World's Top Educators, and *Business Week* called him the best business school professor to teach leadership to executives.

Author of over ninety articles and book chapters and eleven books, he researches leadership, organizational change, boards of directors, and the training and development of leaders and managers. His articles have appeared in the *Harvard Business Review*, *Organizational Dynamics*, *Business & Strategy*, the *Leadership Quarterly*, the *Academy of Management Review*, and the *Journal of Organizational Behavior*. His most recent books include *Shared Leadership* (2002), *Corporate Boards: New Strategies for Adding Value at the Top* (2001), *The Leader's Change Handbook* (1999), *Building Leaders* (1999), and *Winning 'Em Over: A New Model for Management in the Age of Persuasion* (1998). His book *Charismatic*

*Leadership in Organizations* (1998) received the Choice book award. One of his earlier books, *Learning to Lead*, has been described by *Fortune* magazine as "the source" for understanding leadership development.

He has taught at the Harvard Business School, INSEAD (France), the London Business School, McGill University, and the University of Southern California. While a professor at McGill University in Montreal, he received on two occasions McGill's Distinguished Teaching Award. He has received the highest teacher ratings in USC's first-year MBA program. While at the Harvard Business School, he was ranked by first-year MBA students in the top 10 percent of faculty. He is also the recipient of teaching awards from the London Business School. He was awarded by the Center for Creative Leadership their prestigious H. Smith Richardson Fellowship for his research on leadership.

Outside of his work with universities, he consults with a worldwide list of private corporations and nonprofit organizations. A popular speaker and guest on radio and television programs, his insights have been featured in *Business Week*, the *Economist*, the *Financial Times*, *Forbes*, *Fortune*, the *LA Times*, the *New York Times*, the *San Francisco Chronicle*, *Training*, the *Wall Street Journal*, and *Working Woman*.

He received his B.A. from Dartmouth College, his M.B.A. from the University of Virginia, and his D.B.A. from the Harvard Business School. Prior to his academic career, he worked in government and as an international marketing manager for a high technology company.